One Man's Journal

Herbert O'Driscoll

Anglican Book Centre
Toronto, Ontario

3587

Excerpts from the following books are reprinted with permission.

Robert Frost, "The Road Not Taken," *The Poetry of Robert Frost* (New York: Holt, Rinehart and Winston)

Kahlil Gibran, *The Prophet* (New York: Alfred A. Knopf)

Margery Williams, *The Velveteen Rabbit* (New York: Avon Books)

John Masefield, "Cargoes," *Poems* (New York, Macmillan)

1982
Anglican Book Centre
600 Jarvis Street
Toronto, Ontario
Canada M4Y 2J6

Printed in Canada
ISBN 0-919030-89-0

for Niall
who often said good night
while this journal
was being written

Contents

Preface

This journal, once a daily part of many peoples lives, very nearly didn't have a beginning. The idea of a daily radio program seemed too demanding when it was first suggested to me. I felt that the first fifty "pages" of such a journal would be easy, the next fifty would take more thought, the third fifty would be a burden, and the next fifty an agony! What I didn't realize is that life itself, and our living of it, writes our daily journals.

The task of selecting from the pages of a journal, now five years thick, has been difficult. There are so many things that for the present, at least, must remain unshared. In fact, devising categories or themes was not easy; but here they are, simply and straightforwardly named.

My particular thanks go to Ian Alexander, then in charge of radio station CHQM-FM, who persuaded me to begin; to Dave Grierson and John Dritmanis who have recorded the *Journal* for most of its life to this point; to Lesley Godwin who has frequently interpreted my hasty scrawl into typescript for those who wished copies of particular pages.

To say *One Man's Journal* has a philosophy is to burden it too greatly with significance. But I have always written with the realization that many who hear may need what a songwriter vaguely called "an encouraging word." Because of this I have always set out without apology to cheer rather than sadden, to be gentle rather than brutal, to give hope rather than despair. I have not tried to do this because I feel it either desirable or even possible to evade reality. I have tried, even if only by implication, to point to a reality beyond the seeming reality, a music beyond the heard, a meaning beyond the perceived. It is, I suspect, this quality in the *Journal*, rather than any great wisdom or profundity, that has made many ask for a little collection such as this. I hope it will be found an acceptable response.

Vancouver 1981.

Portraits

The ultimate canvas for portraiture is of course one's daily experience. The following selections sometimes describe an actual face, sometimes a fleeting expression seen perhaps in the street or in a hospital corridor. Some of the portraits here are of people known intimately, some are known hardly at all beyond the moment of brief but vivid encounter. Each one is here because for a moment there was communicated to me an inner loveliness or a deeper meaning that simply had to be "painted."

A.Y. Jackson

Among the people who used to go up and down Elgin Street in Ottawa was A.Y. Jackson, then in the last decade of his life. He was short and heavy set, slow moving, quietly spoken, gently smiling. From time to time he would come into the church and sit near the back. I often wondered how eyes like his saw the stained glass windows. Did he feel them pale and stilted in colour and form? I never asked him that at the time. But one thing I did do and I'm very glad now.

One day in the early fall, when the city was basking in one of its two lovely and transient periods of the year which show the capitol at its best, I had an idea. I suggested to A.Y. Jackson that he might like to go for a drive. He had no car and was by that time too old to drive. He said that he would love to go.

We moved through the city, past the Peace Tower and Parliament Hill, down and over the Ottawa River. We began the lovely gentle climb into the Gatineau Hills.

As we drove, the fall colours began to welcome us. We entered wave after wave of reds and golds. The leaves turned and shimmered and danced on the trees. The river, flowing down out of Quebec, was pink in its reflection of the glory along its banks. As the sun lowered in the sky, the tapestry glowed in the way that lasts only a little while before dusk comes.

It was late when we came back. The office homegoing traffic was streaming against us. He was in good form. He had been for a while among the things his art had given to everyone of us in Canada — the lakes, the trees, the hills. And so, as the evening lights shone, I brought A.Y. Jackson home again . . .

A Family Face

I was driving down Cornwall Street the other day. It was about noon on one of those beautiful late fall days. Cornwall is almost dangerous to drive down because you are tempted to glance continually through the gaps in the houses to look at the water and at the mountains.

They came down the sidewalk together. They were going along in the leisurely way that said they were out for a walk. Two women, they walked arm in arm. One was in her early twenties and the other in her late sixties or early seventies. As I passed they paused in their stride, their heads went back almost in unison, and they laughed.

It was one of those flashes that is in a sense very ordinary, and yet it was more. The two women were obviously of the same family. Conceivably they could have been mother and daughter, but I think they may have been grandmother and granddaughter. There was the same style of hair, one dark and the other quite white. There was the same face formation, especially in their shared laughter. In fact for a moment it was as if I had been given a glimpse through a time barrier and had seen the same person alive with laughter at two simultaneous moments of her life. All this flashed into mind as I passed by.

I can't say that I wish to develop any great or profound thought from the incident. There looked to be between them an intimacy and an ease that made time irrelevant. I was also reminded again of the beauty and priceless gift that family relationships can, at their best, give to us. The sharing of laughter, the linking of arms, the similarity of face and stance, all made me aware of the fact that affection knows nothing of time. There can be in family ties such unity that, when eyes look into eyes, they see neither age nor youth, but the reflection of themselves.

The Bicycle Man

The first time I met him, he was stooped over a child's bicycle and was expressing frustration, because whatever he was trying to fix just refused to be fixed. I suppose that's how I always think of him. His hands were usually oily from a thousand bicycles, and he always looked as if he was behind in the mass of work that was constantly accumulating. This was mainly because he found it very hard to say no to small people who wanted their bicycles back as soon as possible.

He began more than a quarter of a century ago in this place. He saw bicycles become an adult hobby after for years being the possession only of the young. He was a blunt man. A spade was a spade. He could be impatient, but with the impatience of someone who was a kind of father figure in the community and was trusted as such, and therefore a grumble was expected and allowed and understood. After all, many who brought their children to the store had themselves stood there as youths.

We stood in the shop recently, the two of us. It was almost a shell. The stock was gone. The shelves and the tools were gathered up, the benches overturned; the building was coming down the following week. He was finishing up. There wouldn't be any more busy Saturdays with broken chains, flat tires, the thrill in a child's eyes as a glittering new bicycle came ticking and gliding out of the downstairs stockroom. We talked for a while about the past and the future, and then we said goodbye.

That was only a couple of weeks ago. The other day I commended him to God as I conducted his funeral. He had had, as they say, "a heart." He went very quickly. I know that medical books don't contain the term "a broken heart." But I think there is such a thing. He laughed a great deal. He had many jokes, and I am very glad that the children and I knew him.

The Old Couple

I had come out of the apartment and had walked across the open area of grass that lies at the end of Davie and Denman Streets and verges on English Bay. It was one of those long evenings of summer that linger in the mind. All around me were people of every age and description. There was a kind of hush in the air, even the car engines seemed muted as the line wound its way home along Beach Avenue, where the yellow bulbs of the popcorn vendors twinkled through the late summer light.

There were family groups, single men and women, couples, all moving about with a kind of weekend relaxation that seemed to savour and extend this hour before nightfall and the beginning of another week.

Among the people, I saw them moving together. They were very old and somewhat bowed, and they moved slowly but in perfect unison arm in arm. It was a rhythm that seemed to come from countless walks together. The long golden road of the sunset flashed them into momentary invisibility as they crossed between it and where I stood. They came to a curb stop at the end of a block. For them it was high. In their fragility, which they had long ceased to disguise, it was a formidable obstacle, even a moment of potential danger.

As I watched, he very slowly stepped into the roadway. When he was safely down, he helped her make the same step carefully and gingerly. Together they set out on the long journey to the other side of the busy street. For them, as for the young couple leaning on the parked car behind me, the sun blazed and the water of the bay moved with all its calm beauty. For them, in their evening, this evening was a taste of beauty. I remembered a phrase of the Bible: "Many waters cannot drown love."

Golden Treasury

It is about eight-thirty in the evening. The eighth floor of the Vancouver General is empty of visitors. Here and there in the corridors a few mobile patients are getting a little bit of exercise before settling down for the night. Two of us are at the end of the corridor chatting. Beside us she is brought out of the room. She is very small and walks very slowly and is supported by a nurse. With help she climbs into a wheel chair. She has grey hair. There is a kind of bird-like fragility to her. From where I stand, I cannot see her face. She is being helped to stay in the wheel chair by a little strap that will prevent her falling forward.

Then the most unlikely thing happens. In a low but strong and perfectly audible voice she begins to recite flowing lines of English poetry. They roll out absolutely unhesitatingly, not a rhyme out of place, not a syllable omitted. It isn't just some accidental clicking in of a long ago memory. Her tone fits the words. After two verses she gives a soft laugh because the young nurse doesn't know what she has recited.

When I walked past her a few minutes later I thanked her. Her face was old, but in it two dark bright eyes looked out in full and intelligent awareness.

Once upon a time there was a benighted and primitive educational system that made people (myself included) learn by heart many great beautiful things. It did this to us so that some day, when we needed a golden treasury to draw upon, we would possess riches within ourselves. The idea was that, however life changed, however far we travelled, whatever befell, we would still have this timeless possession. It would seem that such "memory work" is no longer considered to be good educational practice, and this is to the great loss of a whole generation.

Dalai Lama

In a day or so I shall spend some time in the company of a forty-five year old monk who is at the same time far more than just a monk. He symbolizes one of the world's great religious traditions. For hundreds of thousands of people he embodies in himself an entry point for the divine into the world. I am of course speaking about the Dalai Lama and referring to the fact that he is the spiritual leader of the Tibetan people.

Today I saw him for a moment just a few yards away from me at a press conference. I realize that as he moves from function to function in the city he draws large crowds. For both radio and TV journalists he is very definitely "news." As I look at him, I wonder if there isn't a rather ironic reason for that fascination. I can't help thinking, seeing him face a press conference, that he embodies a particular balance of lifestyles that many in our western society long for wistfully.

There is in the Dalai Lama on the one hand a kind of efficiency and authority, a kind of executive style that we in the West respect and understand. In our language he is very definitely, and seemingly effortlessly, the "chairman of the board." Yet coupled with this is the aura of otherworldliness, a detachment heightened by differences of language and of clothes, and of course inner discipline. Western efficiency and energy mingle with eastern serenity and detachment. We long for that mingling of attributes. There certainly is the realization that two modes of being alive are necessary if we are to function adequately in the extraordinarily demanding world of our time. We will have to cease being a people that is always *doing* and become also a people that is at times merely *being*. This doing and being will have to become a recognized balance in our lives. Indeed who knows? This mingling may one day be seen to have begun in this strange last third of the twentieth century.

One's Own Place

I shall always remember a certain conversation on a certain morning. I remember thinking, that morning, that humanity is very wonderful and can be very beautiful.

She doesn't need a name, although it is very familiar to me as is her remembered face. She was very old and in recent years had become very feeble. As with many people in their senior years she didn't need much sleep, and very often she would go for a walk in the streets of the West End at about five in the morning. She looked as if a puff of wind could blow her away.

There were signs of things happening inside. She began to get a little confused. She would forget where friends lived. She would suddenly drop off for naps. She had a nice little apartment a few floors up, and from it she had a view. Friends began to say that perhaps the time had come to consider going somewhere where there were other people. Quietly the answer was a definite No. Other friends tried. Then I was asked to try.

The arrangement was that we would have a morning cup of tea or coffee in her apartment. When I arrived she took a long time to answer the apartment phone. There was a table for two neatly laid by the window. The room was spotless. We chatted. Slowly we steered toward the subject. Yes, she realized she was slower. Yes, sometimes she did forget things. Yes, she had wonderful friends. Yes, she thought she could carry on. Quiet, gentle, adament.

She carried on for a while because friends kept a close eye. Not very long afterward there was a bit of a fall, and as with everything else, very quietly and gently she did her dying in hospital very much at peace.

I will always remember our morning at that little table. There was a courage and a dignity about her, vulnerable and fragile though she was. To me it seemed to be the human story at its simplest and finest. In her case she won. She stayed in her chosen place, and then, almost it seemed at her own choosing, she left. Somehow everything seemed to have come out all right.

Business Man

Over the last few years we have got to know one another and to respect one another. I think, and I certainly hope, that is mutual. He lives in a very different world from mine. His skills are very different. All his life he has had a real gift for the many intricacies of business and finance. I suppose he would admit ruefully to possessing most of the taken-for-granted attributes to that world. There is an air usually of being a little hurried, perhaps a hesitation, as they say, to accept fools gladly. There is the neat dark suit, the brisk walk, which places him eternally between the last appointment and the next one, the briefcase with its ever bulging papers, those white sacramental signs of our wrestlings in the market place.

In that same market place, in its corridors and offices and airplanes and board rooms, I happen to know that he is honourable and generous. Once I listened to him in another situation. Both the place and the language were different. He was sharing what we had all agreed to call each other's journey of faith. The language he used was very simple sometimes. He spoke of being taught, and of never forgetting, the words of the hymn "Jesus loves me, this I know, for the Bible tells me so." He spoke of learning other words likewise remembered which said, "We have an anchor which keeps the soul, firm and strong, when the billows roll."

These are, as I said, simple things. You might say, if you were in a critical mood, that they are childish things. And yet, as we know, to possess such roots can be beyond value. That's what someone else meant when he said many centuries ago, "Except ye become as little children, ye cannot see the kingdom of heaven."

Victory

The human face is a wonderful thing. I sometimes think it is a kind of country, or rather the map of a country. Sometimes it indicates beauty and peace, other times terror and pain, with endless refinements and variations between.

I am sitting on a bed in a room. We are facing each other, he on a chair with one leg supported on a stool. We are having a very slow conversation, sometimes waiting for him to concentrate with all his might on a word that refuses to come, a sentence that refuses to be completed. Sometimes, as he struggles, I can see the pain and frustration in his eyes.

He is among the people whom, I suspect, I will always remember however long I live. In medical terms he has been through a great deal. In terms of the interior life he possesses resources that must be deep and immense. Without them the medical resources would long since have been of little avail.

As I sit here, I am suddenly aware that immediately above him is his own photograph. He gazes out from it, handsome and smiling, in the officer's uniform of a now long ago war. That face has all the smoothness and firmness and line of youth. Underneath it he now sits. The living face, this face I now see, is ravaged by a battle for life more magnificent than any military battle. It is a life lived with laughter and courage and tenacity over the last decade. It is a life which will continue to look out of those eyes as he once again gains strength and coherence.

Two faces — one handsome and untested, the other lined but so totally magnificent.

Birthday

We gathered to celebrate a birthday. There were some usual things — cake, sparklers, small presents, small children wide-eyed with the light of the sparklers reflected in their eyes. But this was different. We had come to celebrate ninety years of somebody's life, and I had been given the honour, though I was not part of the family, to propose the toast.

We made some jokes, the good natured intimate easy jokes of such an occasion. Elderly friends sat on chairs around the walls of the room. The women of the family and their grown-up daughters moved efficiently in and out of the kitchen, producing a wealth of good things. Small grandchildren and even great-grandchildren moved in and out between people's legs.

At the centre of it all he stood. Sometimes he sat when he needed to rest. He was deeply happy. He made a speech. It spoke of long ago memories and far away places. It moved along roads of quiet recollection mentioning love experienced and things accomplished, a few might-have-been choices. It told of a full and long life to this point. On that long road there had been a contribution made at every level of life — to the country, to the province, to the community, to a loving family.

It wasn't a dramatic occasion. It was quiet and gentle, a domestic moment. Yet I mention it because it was lovely and gracious. It linked the past with the present. It spoke of a fulfilled and whole person. I watched him as he responded to the toast, his hand shaped by a long ago wound in the war, and I thought of the simple lines of a poet:

like a white candle
in a holy place,
so is the beauty
of an aged face.
(Padraic Colum)

Dancing Home

I remember once reading a remark of that very gifted man Lewis Thomas, who writes so fascinatingly about science. I like him because he writes in a way that I can understand about things that are technically quite beyond me. His classic work is, I think, entitled *The Lives of a Cell.*

Lewis Thomas once said that the ultimate mystery is life itself — the fact of being alive, the quality we know as "aliveness." We can see it, experience it, tend it when ill; but the quality itself is, and probably always will be, the ultimate mystery. Sometimes we come to realize its wonder in a terrible way when we suddenly see it go from a person or from anything living.

I thought of aliveness the other day. I was standing in a ward in a suburban hospital, standing at the end of the bed. The early spring sun was flooding in and making her hair gleam on the pillow. She was lying on her side, preparing to have her rest for the day. Moving was not easy because there had been a fall followed by a hip operation.

She is a tiny person. She told me how she fell. She was outside her house and it was such a lovely day that she had looked up into the endless blue to say a thank-you for all the beauty. Then she had fallen. As she told me this she chuckled, her eyes danced at the irony of it all, and in her voice was not a trace of fear or despondency.

She is 96, and her mind echoes with music and dancing. She brought folk dancing and the teaching of it to this west coast nearly three quarters of a century ago. Her mind and body and spirit will possess music and dance as long as she breathes. Her doctors say that she is healing magnificently. As I left to allow her to rest, which incidentally she showed no signs of doing, she touched the hip which had been mended and said, "Don't breathe a word to anybody, but I'm going to dance all the way home."

So she will, because in her is the endless and unsilencable music of the mystery we call life.

Fisherman

It was in early September and it was the last hour or so of one of those evenings of late summer when the sun, low on the horizon, pours in from the gulf and touches every ripple of high tide water by Spanish Banks. In that hour there are people who do slow and lazy things and move along the beaches.

He was moving in and out of the water in his great thigh-high fishing boots. There was a bucket on the beach behind him, and when I saw him he was about twenty feet out, the water nearly to his chest as he smoothed and settled his nets. He moved slowly as if he had all of time. He worked easily and with the sureness of years of experience. A few people watched him, some speaking, some not. Then he came out of the water and put some fish in the bucket, and a woman with a dog said something to him.

They were both middle-aged to elderly, she with head-scarf, naturally pale, fine-boned, dressed precisely, leading a dog on a leash. He was a dark ruddy golden man, face heavy but strong, deeply lined, eyes crinkled, cigarette held with the lips, expansive in gesture. He was telling her that he lived with his son. He said that he was Greek. That he was not long in Canada, but that he was very very happy. That he had fished all his life, and that now he loved to do it here in the evening when the sun shone.

As I heard the thin precise English voice and the deep broken sentences laughing together, I was aware of a moment of *shalom*. There was the setting sun, there were two worlds meeting, there was age and maturity and experience and contentment. Yet even with these words I have still not captured the essence of that golden moment.

Post Office

I have watched him for the last few years. The way I see him has changed because I have got to know him very slightly over the years. He still fascinates me, particularly during the days of the Christmas rush.

He is, I would say, in his senior years of employment, and by and large he has a sad face. He stands behind the counter of the Post Office and presides over an annual madness that he now views with a kind of Olympian calm. I have seen others trying to do his job. They face the line of unmailed parcels — all awaiting stamps, custom slips, first class stickers, air mail stickers — and their faces pale and their hands fumble, their foreheads glisten and their voices attain a high nervous pitch.

With my friend it is quite different. He obviously has a system. He has accepted that for a few days the world will go mad. Otherwise intelligent human beings will buy one stamp when they should buy twenty. Some will be unable to fill out a green form two inches square without six questions. Others will want to know the different cost of mailing parcels depending on which one of ten categories they decide to avail themselves. My friend knows all that can be known. He knows all the ways, all the options, all the possibilities. He is stern but never unjust. He exudes authority tempered by mercy. Particularly stupid questions or arguments are dealt with summarily. His voice is deep, at times even gruff, but he never smiles. Mind you there are moments when I have seen his facial muscles move as if about to draw back and reveal his bared teeth, but he has always managed to refrain. I suspect that he is a kind of Obi Wan Ben Kenobi, one of a cadre of Jedi knights that the Post Office keeps in reserve to hurl into the fray when the battle is at its worst. God bless them, or should I say, "May the force be with them . . ."

Touch

I waited in the corridor as the physiotherapy sessions began to break up before lunch in the rooms and wards. The wheel chairs came, the walkers passed, the elevators whirred. And then I went to find him.

We had known each other for a few years. No great intimacy really. We had worked together. He had had a stroke. He was sitting in the chair when I went in. I did the things we all do. I smiled. But of course the gift of smiling is taken away sometimes by a stroke. You realize how large an area of communicating it robs a person of. I spoke a few words of greeting. But of course conversation is sometimes taken too, and you realize how much you take for granted in life. I bent down and tried to get our eyes to meet. But those "windows of the soul," as they have been called, can become temporarily shuttered and dim by a blow such as this. So we sat there opposite each other. Then I bent forward and placed my hand in the upturned curve of his fingers. Slowly they closed on my hand. I felt the warmth of him and the struggling for life and the unspoken words and the searching of dimmed eyes and the laughter on lips that will, please God, one day at a time, find life again. Then some lunch came, and I said goodbye and left.

Ranch Lady

I had promised that sometime during the holidays we would go horseback riding, and as it was a family promise, I was held to it. So one day we turned into the driveway where the road takes a turn, and then we were at the ranch. We had been here before, and there was excitement and anticipation. But the main interest to me was to watch somebody at work.

I don't know her name. She has a nick name stitched to her jacket so that visitors can identify her, but I won't say it, at least not yet. I suspect she has been in charge of things here for a number of years. She looks and acts like a professional.

It seems to be her life's task, with some assistance, to look after this ranch of some forty horses. Each day she directs the assembling of children, adults, and horses. She has to work very fast. She moves quickly and decisively with great nervous energy. She is a small person tanned from the sun, her hair short and practical but attractive, and when she mounts a horse the two become one, because she is so obviously at home in the saddle. What struck me was the gentleness and care she brings to something she does day after day. Gentleness and care is given to both horses and humans. Every horse is called by name. Every child is spoken to. Every stirrup is carefully tightened, quick items of interest about horses are dropped here and there as she moves in and out of the assembling group. There is an impressive mingling of someone capable, enthusiastic, essentially caring. Perhaps that's why the nick name on her shirt is simply "Maw." She is one of the faces and voices I find myself being grateful for.

Wood Carver

He is in the workshop when we find him. He is a tall man, now stooped, yet his frame is large and powerful. He is patriarchal, a thick mop of grey hair swept back, a heavy equally grey beard. At a certain distance down his nose is perched a pair of glasses that somehow seem to be out of proportion to the rest of him. He stands by his work bench clad in heavy sweater, trousers to the knee, and heavy socks so common to this area of Germany. When he speaks in English his voice is very low and heavily accented.

He has always lived in this village of Oberammergau. He is now in his extremely active upper seventies. All his life he has, in different ways, taken part in the drama with which this place has been totally involved for over three centuries. He recalls a time before the present vast theatre. He first became part of the cycle of the great Passion Play as a very small child in 1910. By now he has been involved in the drama eight times including the Jubilee performance of 1934. He tells in a remembering voice of the various parts he has been given over the years. He has played many roles. First one of the children in the play, then a member of the crowd scenes, later a friend of Jesus, after that Pilate, and later still Herod. This year he plays what is presumably his last role, again that of Herod.

The play and woodcarving have been his life. To look at him one cannot help feeling that it has been a good life. I hear it in his voice. I wanted to share with you the contentment that came from him.

Wounded Healer

I suppose it is the nature of things that into any one's journal some accidents and sickness must come. For two weeks we tasted the joy of a lakeside cottage. Then the accident. In itself I suppose it is incidental, but I was grateful for the insights that came as I moved through it.

In one sentence what happened was that I slipped on a dock one stormy day and broke my wrist. There followed a day and a half in hospital. In hospital and in sickness our minds are more than usually sensitive to the attitudes of others toward us. More than all the rest one person comes to my mind. I don't know her name, but that doesn't matter. My first impression, as she came into the waiting room and called my name, was an impression of kindness and friendliness and, for some reason, weariness. She is, I would say, in her early sixties, her hair greyish, straight, neat. When she asked me to follow her, I noticed that she moved slowly with a tentative, slightly lurching walk. As she asked me to prepare for the X-ray, she chatted gently and reassuringly. Her voice was quiet, her accent English. Then, as she placed my arm in the correct position on the machine, I saw her fingers, delicate, spotlessly clean, already twisted in the unmistakable contours of arthritis.

I suppose it was the way she tended myself and others. She not only witnessed pain, but obviously experienced it with grinding persistency. I could not help but see her as a kind of wounded healer. And precisely because she was wounded it gave her a sympathy and gentleness that communicated itself in every word and touch. I was very moved.

Odette

I have just met a fascinating person. Before I chat about her, I want to talk about a type. There is a certain kind of human being that I think of as peculiarly English, although for all I know she has her equivalent in other lands and other societies. But I suspect not. I suspect she was created by a certain period of history and a certain kind of society. For some reason I think of her as elderly but somehow unbelievably spry. She is for some reason in my mind rather small but tough as nails. Not tough in language — really quite gentle and well spoken. But the impression is given that she could be tough very quietly, if only for the fact that she doesn't know what fear is.

Well, I've met her (as a type of course) before, and lo and behold, I met her again in an apartment beside Stanley Park. She has been (they always are) travelling all over the world, not on a gleaming cruise liner to sunny ports with westernized hotels, but to some of the lonely places of the earth. In fact, because of those travels she is a world authority on the strange elusive creature that is sought all over the mountainous regions of mainly the northern hemisphere, and that we in the north west of the continent call Sasquatch.

My acquaintance is not at all a crank. She has at least four serious books to her credit by well known publishers. She has worked and travelled with people like Lord Hunt, who conquered Everest. She corresponds with serious scientists around the world, attended the recent conference at the University of British Columbia, and is an absolutely fascinating person to meet. Yet to meet her in the West End that day you would have thought she would be nervous to cross Denman Street. But she talks with intimacy and affection about the Hindu Kush Range, and her elderly eyes, reflected in the small teacup, have seen places I shall never go to. Meeting her was a very special experience . . .

Jimmy

His name isn't Jimmy. It's like that but it isn't, and it doesn't matter. You often see Jimmy because there are many of him around the city. You see him sometimes walking very purposefully in the downtown area. It's the pitifully purposeful walk you notice in so many men who have nowhere to go. Oh yes, sometimes there is a destination. There is the cheque that means survival. Sometimes it comes from half forgotten people or an unknown lawyer's office and a long ago estate, but most often it comes from some level of government. Or there is the walk to a clinic for this or that, where you sit with others and chew the fat and the doctor cuts your story short because you've told it so often and it's become more complex and more rambling.

And sometimes with some Jimmys there are the days that become no-days, the times out of time when you wake with a vague memory of things done, people met and lost again, resolutions broken and money spent. And after those days, when you know it's now a matter of survival for a while, you think of the places you just might be welcome if you found somebody in the right mood, where you might be acknowledged to be just you without questions or sermons. And you set out, and you do the rounds. And sometimes you're lucky and sometimes not.

Then there are Jimmy's dreams. The high days. The breakthroughs. There will all of a sudden be a job. It's going to be steady. The boss has made promises about the future. There may even be the promise of training. Or there may be a far away dream. I remember Jimmy when he was going to Calgary. There was a job. This was it. And as you see Jimmy over the years you learn that the dreams must not be shattered, the breakthroughs not dismissed as unreal. Because they are Jimmy's only reality. And when the dream is over and he sits with a cut forehead in the hall, you make some coffee and you never say, "I told you so."

On Being 85

The trouble with most famous last words is that they are very rarely worth their fame. Frequently they are either contrived or fatuous. But there is a variation on famous last words. It comes when the very old are asked to surmise why they have had such a long life.

I have seen endless varieties of reply to this question and can remember none. But the other day I came across the kind of reply that makes you want to meet the person who said it. I don't know if what she said was triggered by any questions. I do know that she was 85 years old. This is what she said.

"If I had my life to live over, I would dare to make more mistakes next time. I'd relax. I would limber up. I would be sillier than I have been this trip. I would take fewer things seriously. I would take more chances. I would take more trips. I would climb mountains. I would eat less beans and more ice cream. I would perhaps have more active troubles, but I would have fewer meager ones.

"You see, I'm one of those people who live sensibly and sanely year after year, day after day. Oh, I've had my moments, and if I had it to do over again, I'd have more of them. Just moments, one after another, instead of living so many years ahead of each day. I've been one of those persons who never goes anywhere without a thermometer, a hot water bottle, a raincoat, and a parachute. If I had it to do over, I would travel much lighter. If I had my life to live over, I would start barefoot earlier in the spring, and stay that way later in the fall. I would go to more dances. I would ride more merry-go-rounds."

Her name is Nadine Stair, and she lives in Lexington, Kentucky. As I said, she sounds the kind of person one would like to meet.

Terry Fox

Across this vast country we live in there runs a highway that, were it not so familiar and taken for granted, would be one of the world's wonders. I'm referring of course to the Trans Canada Highway. Many months ago on the eastern coast, where that highway meets the grey Atlantic, a boy turned his magnificent body toward the western horizon and began to walk.

His body had been by that time the focus of two forces. First it had been attacked by what is perhaps the greatest enemy of our physical humanity. Because of that enemy a limb had been removed, with all the immense trauma that that alone entails. But, as well, that body had been brought to a high level of fitness by the immense inner discipline and strength that made this young man the giant he was.

He set out on a journey that in reality involved two great highways. One was the great wide road that spans this family of provinces called Canada. The other highway was a more terrible and darker one, the highway of physical agony and ever-present exhaustion which he had to experience. One highway was full of companionship, cars, crowds, cameras, friends. The other highway he had to walk alone. You cannot share pain or weariness.

Today we celebrate the completion (in the deepest sense of that word) of that great journey. There is in the New Testament a statement made to another young man. It says simply this. "I have fought a good fight. I have finished the course. I have kept the faith." Paul said this to Timothy in a letter now part of the New Testament. It could be said of Terry Fox.

There are circumstances where you suddenly become aware of human scale. I think of two moments, each in relation to the Trans Canada Highway. One moment was experienced while looking down on part of that highway from a plane window and seeing the insect-like crawl of a car moving far below. From where one sat one could see the endless miles rolling ahead on the thin shining ribbon, and one realized the utter slowness of the tiny machine.

The other moment came while having dinner on that same highway. I noticed how at ground level it diminished a human being. In almost every province there are some wide and empty vistas rolling away from the highway, dwarfing anyone who walks beside it, making them feel their walking is achieving nothing, so huge is the natural stage on which they move.

Down this endless highway and across this vast stage has moved a young man. He not only challenged the crushing scale of it all, but he challenged what must have been a white fire of pain in his body igniting with every movement. There must have been moments when he felt dwarfed to insignificance under the vault of the sky and the ocean of concrete. There must have been moments when he felt himself immobilized even while he walked, reaching for an ever receding horizon.

Yet, of course, not only was Terry Fox not diminished; instead he taught us that there can be a glory to our humanity which is beyond all consideration of size or scale. Far from being dwarfed, he walked the land as a giant.

It is extraordinary how powerful can be the influence of a single human being. They do not have to possess even the outward look of power. Yet there come occasions when from that person there pours out an influence that has ramifications far beyond them. Their words or their actions are like a tiny pebble which when dropped into great lake creates ever widening circles of effect.

One cannot help thinking of men and women who in a strange way possessed the power of non-power — to put it paradoxically. Francis, small, insignificant, given to laughter in long ago Assisi, yet able to walk through an army of Moslem spears. Ghandi, almost a figure of fun to some, tiny, emaciated, yet moulding many millions of people into a great subcontinent. Teresa, a slight Croation woman, not beautiful as we tend to judge beauty, but walking like a queen through hellish places of human suffering.

I am thinking of course of another human being. Not possessing powers as we measure it, he was proved to be the possesser of very great power. He was given the power to move what seemed an impossible hope into an amazing reality. That power moved millions of people to respond in a way many had never responded before. He became the focus of that dangerous friend, the public media, and yet retained absolute integrity. In the face of indescribable pain toward the end of each day's terrible journey, he was given the power to overcome. As we think of Terry Fox, we find it difficult to deny that there is available to us a power beyond our own. But each of us has to decide and to discover that mystery.

Today this vast country of ours, divided by so many things, is as near to becoming one as it can be. It is divided by geography into regions, by history into provinces, by economics into have and have-not provinces, by culture and language into two worlds, and by our recent discovery of resources, into power structures that wrestle with one another in secluded boardrooms and parliamentary committees.

Yet across all these divisions a boy has walked. In his journey he has, by his life and death, by much suffering and magnificent courage, forged a unity in the fleeting hours of a particular day in our history.

Throughout that day Terry Fox is remembered and commended to God. This is done in uncounted ways, by individuals in their solitude, by communities through which he once passed, by towns and villages and cities which he never knew. The words are in many languages, the symbols are of the world's great traditions, but in their intention and by the focus of their thoughts, millions of Canadians are, for that day, one.

This sense of unity, with its focus on a young man's life and death, is a witness to the immense and mysterious power of our individual humanity. It is more powerful in its effect than laws, governments, constitutions. It moves us deeply, far more deeply than any of these things I have mentioned, almost as if speaking through the human spirit is another and greater spirit. The Bible speaks of that as the image of God.

Discoveries

There are moments when one learns something. The something learned is not mere information but rather insight. A word said, a face turned, a figure approaching, a familiar scene looked at one more time. Suddenly a door of the mind is opened and another country is glimpsed. And even though the door closes again, what has been revealed remains and reverberates in the mind.

Sunset

It is about eight o'clock of an evening in these summer weeks. It is an hour when the city is lingering over a drowsy golden day. I have just given two people Holy Communion in an apartment high over English Bay. As I walk back to the car, carrying the small leather container for the Bread and Wine, I walk through all the movement of this area where city and bay meet. People of every age are here. Along the road by the beach the cars move slowly, full of families and couples. The young couples with the first faintly yellowing hair of bronzed summertime, the families with tired children enjoying the first of this year's endless evenings of childhood.

Far out over the inlet and the surrounding hills the sun is setting. I realize that more and more people are beginning to pause in their evening walk. The car parked behind me has a young couple leaning on its roof and looking west. Out there is the largest and loveliest golden and scarlet falling asleep of the sun I have ever seen.

Once ten years ago I journeyed south from Athens to Cape Sunion and stood in the ruins of the temple, there to watch the sun go down over the Mediterranean. Yet this sun, setting on a younger ocean, at least younger in our memories and civilization, is more terrible and, if there can be such an expression, more royal.

A man stood beside me as I looked. He suddenly said, "Isn't that something else?" The reason why it was much more than a commonplace remark was that he was moved to say something, anything, to a complete stranger. The reason he was moved, the reason why we all turned — old, young, drivers, pedestrians — the reason was that we were all, whether we knew it or not, on the edge of worship.

Voyager

It is strange how sometimes a piece of information can intrigue and haunt one for a reason that is very hard to put into words.

In the last couple of years we have put two machines into space. Maybe what is a bit special about them is that, unlike most of our products for space, they will never come back. We designed them that way. We called them Voyager 1 and Voyager 2, and they have already given us some mind-boggling photographs and done some devastating things to some theories we had about the rest of the solar system.

At this moment Voyager 1 is moving along in the gulf that lies between the two greatest planets in our system, Jupiter and Saturn. Eventually it will be drawn into Saturn's orbit, and after that it will be flung like a stone from a catapult out to the edge of the solar system. By September of the year 1989 Voyager 1 will flash by Neptune, that last of the Sun's planets, and then it will begin its endless journey across an unimaginable void between us and the next star system.

We have a hope, a fragile hope some feel it to be, that some time in some infinitely distant future Voyager 1 may come among other life and other minds. In case that should ever happen, we have placed in Voyager 1 some messages which may speak about us. Among them is a recording of the Cavatina from Beethoven's Quartet in B Major Opus 130. Some feel that it is the greatest evocation of human sorrow ever expressed. It intrigues me to think of it out there, a voice of our deepest humanity, a kind of cry among the stars . . .

Symbols of Order

I watched her as she sat on the horse, motionless while it stood, then moving her body easily and gracefully with the movements of the horse as it stepped slowly forward. Behind her, sometimes before her, and sometimes even all around her, the hundreds of toy-like soldiers moved. Over them all the grey leaden skies of London lumbered by. It was the Queen's birthday.

I asked myself why? Why is it all done? It means nothing in any practical tangible terms. It no longer guards anything. Behind it all there are, in Britain, some terrifying practical problems and crises. Does it fly in the teeth of all that is sane?

Let me share a reason why all this pageantry may one day be seen as the sanest possible thing.

Human life is always lived on a kind of vulnerable island between order and chaos, sanity and madness. We live in an age when the conditions of insecurity and complexity make the fabric of human society, and indeed the inner human psyche, very fragile. Chaos — personal, communal, social, financial, international — seem in many ways to be very near. In such a world it is important that we affirm a belief that has lifted humanity, for better or for worse, from the cave to today. It is the belief that, in spite of all the sometimes terribly contrary evidence, the universe has order and design. One of the ways to act this out is *liturgy*, either religious or secular. Actually, at the deepest level, all liturgy is religious. Whether it be that line of sheepish officials following a piper to the head table of yet another convention, or whether it be a nervous girl making her way up an aisle to her wedding, or May Day in Moscow, or somebody carrying the city mace into the council chamber in our own city — every one of these seemingly unnecessary things makes an affirmation that there exists an order, a design, a meaning in the jumbled reality of contemporary life.

Wrong Number

Something simple happened recently that made me think a great deal. The funny thing was that I was aware of the situation in theory, but when I came across an example of it, I was struck very vividly by its intensity.

I had meant to place a long distance call to Toronto. To save money I wanted to do it before eight in the morning. I suddenly realized it was a minute or two before the hour; so I very quickly dialled the number. The moment I heard a child's voice on the other end, I knew I had made a mistake. However, just in case, I asked if that was such and such a place, and there was a puzzled silence. Then the child said that it was not Toronto. So I was about to hang up when I thought I would rescue something; so I asked if I could speak to her mother. A woman came on the phone, very careful, edgey, rather suspicious. I asked her what city it was. No reply. I asked her again. Very grudgingly she said, "Wisconsin." I explained that I had meant to get Toronto. Could she give me the area code of Wisconsin? Grudgingly she gave it. Then I asked, so that I could report my mistake, if she would give me their number. I didn't ask for any name. No, she thought I should speak to her husband. The husband came on in a tone that was really asking, What the hell is going on here? I told my story, asked him if he would give me their number. First there was a hesitation; then he said he couldn't as it was unlisted. I retired defeated.

It was a sad revealing of something hard to express. I was obviously a mysterious undefined threat. I was an unseen enemy to be on guard against. This voice that had entered into their lives had to be silenced. When it was silenced, presumably the anxious and threatened privacy could be recovered. I had a creepy feeling that if I had been pleading for help the result would be the same. I had a feeling that I had experienced not so much an incident displaying individual alienation, as something which to some degree we all experience.

Ultra Sound

We are standing, the three of us, in a room in one of the pavilions of the Vancouver General Hospital. All of us in our different positions are looking at a small screen. It shows a dim and shadowed landscape which is both infinitely far away and yet literally within reach.

Of the two people with me, one is a doctor and the other is a woman joyfully expecting her child. What we are looking at now is her child. It is as yet unborn and lying in the womb. On the screen we are looking into that mysterious planet occupied by its single inhabitant, an infinitely fragile yet strong womb, a city with one all important citizen. Indeed the womb is more a palace housing a king or queen for whom we, at the moment, are the surrounding and supportive courtiers.

We watch, and the mother laughs softly with joy as that tiny inhabitant acts out a part on the screen. We can see the heart beating. We can see a leg being drawn up, an arm waving as if that other life in that other inner universe were in some sense aware of our observation and were sending a greeting to us. We even see that tiny thumb find its way to the mouth and begin to suck.

The three of us are sharing a mystery. Of course we can explain it. We have a jargon for this technology. We call it "ultra sound." But knowing the facts does not in any way diminish the wonder of what we have seen . . .

Two Trees

At the back of our house there are three sets of windows. From any one of these windows you can see two huge living things, two trees. They are part of the family, not intruding but always there, standing mute but vast, silent yet in their way communicating.

They are very different, these two old friends. One is a high straight hemlock tree. Thickly branched, wide at the base, slender as you go higher, it moves to the wind in slow undulations. In its inner reaches — and it is difficult to see deeply into it because of its thick covering — it seems to remain still even in the wind, rather as the ocean depths are still even when the surface is heaving.

The other tree is a cherry tree. It is far less shaped, standing with wide open branches that hide nothing of its limbs. One tree looks strong, protected, private, solid, unchanging. The other is open, gentle, vulnerable, changing. Right now the tall hemlock is as massive as it was in winter. On the other hand winter saw the cherry tree naked, gaunt, pitiable, a thing of sadness and death. But now her branches, the odd one stretching almost to the house window in an attempt to draw attention, are bursting with a white and green trembling loveliness. Death is departing, and life is flowing back through her and clothing her limbs.

The great hemlock is almost contemptuous. In the face of this mercurial change, this vulnerability, this rhythm of nakedness and clothing, this reaching for life and eventual sinking to death again, the hemlock offers instead permanence, stolidity, consistency.

Yet, if it can be said that we have feelings for trees, I find that, while I respect and admire the hemlock, I love the cherry tree. I suspect it is because the tide of life that pulses in her beauty has the glory and fragility of humanity.

The Rider

Judging by our own children I would say that she was fourteen. First, however, a word about the day. It was one of those days when one year spends some time in ending and another year is going through the process of beginning. They say that it all happens in the few minutes before and after midnight on 31 December, but of course that is nonsense. At least from Christmas Eve to about the end of the first week in January, time is changing for us all in a hundred ways, whether or not we are aware of it. It doesn't matter what one is doing; even if one is back at the office, there is an inbetweenness about that couple of weeks. They are time outside of ordinary time. We betray this in little ways. We say to each other, "Happy New Year," for as long as we can stretch it as a salutation. We sign cheques dated in the old year when we mean the new year. We are in a No Man's Land between the two halves of winter.

And so it was that, in this strange time out of time, I was driving along Garden City Way in Richmond. It was cold and clear, the clarity that comes to the coast seldom enough for us to remark on it. And suddenly she came toward me up the Boulevard on a white horse. Because my window was open and it was early in the morning of a holiday, I heard the hooves strike the earth. The rider's hair flew behind her. Suddenly the lights changed, and we both set our steed onward again, mine a grubby and undignified Mini, hers a lively skittish animal.

I looked in the rear-view mirror as she galloped away into the morning sunlight, and saw beyond her the distant mountains. Days have gone by, and now I am not sure whether I saw a suburban child on a horse probably given as a season's present, or whether it was a princess allowing herself to be visible for a moment to a mere mortal, as she rode from the ocean to a distant land beyond the mountains . . .

Visitor

It was just at that point in the Mass or Eucharist where the Gospel had been read and there is about to be a short homily or sermon. As I took the microphone I heard the voice. At first it was timid and far-off, and then it grew stronger.

Standing in the gallery she was outlined against the light of the large west windows. I could not see her face. Her voice sounded that of a girl in her early twenties. There was silence in the Cathedral. Only the two of us, very far away from each other, were involved in this sudden and unplanned encounter.

She wished, she said, to tell us all, to tell the world, of the experience and exultation which she felt. She had composed a song because she felt that was the only way. Her body swayed and gesticulated in her anxiety and urgency. I asked her if she could wait until afterward, and I and others would listen to her song. She couldn't possibly wait. She had to do it and leave. So I said that she could sing her song, and she began.

It was not so much a song as a chant. The words and phrases were hesitant but understandable. After a little while the cries sank to silence and her body stopped swaying and gesticulating, and it was over. She was satisfied. So the Eucharist moved on, its music a Mass setting of a long ago century.

But she stayed in my mind as a symbol of the intensity of contemporary society, of its deep hunger for experience of the transcendent. There is a wide spectrum to be seen today, varying from deep psychological illness to genuine and ennobling spiritual discovery. I don't know where on that spectrum she was, because she was gone before I could meet her. But her voice cried of all the strain and lostness and searching that our strange age knows so well. For this reason it is perhaps fitting that I can give her no name.

Parable

You have very probably had this kind of experience. You see something. It may only last a fleeting second. But for some reason it triggers something in your mind. And when you come to put form on it — to say why it intrigued you, what feelings it created in you, and why — you find it almost impossible to define what the fleeting image communicated.

It was a hilly street, fairly wide. At each side were grass patches before you stepped on to the sidewalk. There were trees. Under the trees were a few parked cars. It was a spring day, with all the mixture of light and shadow of spring. And there was a breeze suddenly there, then gone, and suddenly there again. And on the edge of the side of the road were two small children.

It was one of those lovely sad days of spring when the Japanese cherry trees have held their glory for a short while and then are robbed of it all, and it carpets the ground for a fleeting time. And on this day the petals had just fallen. The two children would gather them in their tiny hands, and then in an ecstasy of abandonment, they would straighten up and raise their arms to the windy sky, open wide their palms and away the petals would go.

Near the children was a parked car. Little by little its outline was disappearing under a covering of pink petals. They clung to the gleaming surface, clustering in bunches wherever they fell. And suddenly I realized that this was an image of what all mankind is trying to do. We are trying to cloak technology and discipline it, and transform it to the patterns of nature. We are trying to make the technical and the natural friends not enemies. And two small children would never know that they were acting out a parable . . .

Two Songs

I am sitting in the back seat of the car. In the front is one of my family with her boy friend. They have a tape on. It is a tape of John Denver, and since I like John Denver, I let down the auditory defences that I have developed to most of the tapes that most of my family play. Mind you, to develop auditory defences to some contemporary music is no mean feat, considering it assaults you with all the ferocity of Attila and his legendary Huns. However, I must be reasonable. There are some lovely ballads to be heard these days.

I find myself intrigued by a line of Denver's song. He sings, "I feel the power of everything I see." He sings it high and with great passion. It sums up a great deal about a certain kind of religiousity of our time. There is among many people a sense of being in tune or wishing to be in tune with the world we live in. It takes many forms. Walking barefoot in a field to experience the earth. Listening to silence. It's almost as if a whole generation, not sure what or who to believe, are saying that there is a reality out there, a voice trying to get through, a hand trying to reach out to touch our humanity. I am reminded of another poet who over a century and a half ago wrote what John Denver is now singing. That poet, walking in the lovely Lake District of England, sang

I have felt
A presence that disturbs me with the joy
Of elevated thoughts; a sense sublime
Of something far more deeply interfused
Whose dwelling is the light of setting suns,
And the round ocean and the living air,
And the blue sky, and in the mind of man
A motion and a spirit, that impels
All thinking things, all objects of all thought
And rolls through all things.

Friendship

This is a special day. Millions of children went back to school today, and with them another summer moved into memory. By this time in the day some are beginning to enjoy the rest of the day because they have been let out early. This lovely sunlit afternoon will be an extra, an afternoon of play snatched from the arms of duty, hours of delight grasped on the edge of weeks of diligence and discipline.

I am coming down from the university. It is mid-afternoon. The grass of the boulevard is green and shimmering after yesterday's rain. Two small boys are doing what small boys have done since Shakespeare wrote about them. They are punctuating the journey home with various side activities. As I come nearer they end wrestling and begin the process of preparing to cross the second half of the avenue. They stand torn between the seriousness of letting my car go by and the fun of touching each other, arm twisting and pushing and shoving, which is a kind of extension of their wrestling. They are tousleheaded. The sun shines on their hair, probably washed this morning at the insistence of two unseen and unsung mothers. They are laughing as I leave them behind.

They do not know it, but they are engaged in another journey. They are discovering something that one day they will realize is even more precious than the knowledge they have been taught in school. It is something nobody can teach them. They are on this journey home discovering the gift of friendship.

Ottawa

Around the airport the countryside is flat. It is actually a kind of low plateau of land southwest of the City. You could be almost anywhere. When you enter the main area of the airport there really is nothing to tell you that you are in a very special place. The city is not like other capital cities, if we are sensitive to these things.

You get a taxi and it heads in through the drab countryside that slopes north to the distant river. After a while you come to the first houses. Like many subdivisions they bear a name that tries to conjure up a bygone age, a rural lifestyle. You see on a hoarding, "Modern Country Living at Hunt Club Chase."

Then you see the city spread across the as yet low skyline in front of you. There are very few features. Even when you have looked a long time, and incidentally only if you know where to look, you see it. The great grey granite column topped by the clock and the roof of copper turning green. You realize that it is the Peace Tower and that beneath it are the Parliament buildings and this is Ottawa, the country's capital.

Slender was the word that came to my mind as I searched for the Peace Tower and lost it again, while we swept into the city area. How slender our national symbols are, how few and far between, how timid, how almost apologetic. Even with the symbols we have, we are a little diffident, almost embarrassed. We are not good at flag waving or the playing of anthems. We are relatively unimpressed by public figures, and only rarely are we given to speeches about Canada. The Americans are much better at all that. They are rich in symbols, and they use them and enjoy them. There are worse vices than pride in one's country. We are, I think, going to need all that we can muster in the years to come . . .

Journeys in Canada

Perhaps to choose a country, rather than to be born in it, creates an even stronger bond. These journeys have taken me across the vastness and variety of this country, allowing me to savour its many terrains and different moods. Usually at some stage in each journey there has been a period of quietness in which to savour the place, to capture, if you will, the spirit that dwells there.

Morning City

I came down Burrard Street, down the series of terraced hills that drop from Sixteenth Avenue, down past the brewery and onto the bridge. It was very early, about six-thirty in the morning, and the traffic was still quite sparse. Suddenly I realized that it was one of those mornings of special and rare beauty.

My little Mini began to cross the bridge. In a Mini you are low down, and I have discovered that from it you look through the stone railings of the bridge, and this changes the quality of the light of everything you see. The sun, which hung over Mt Baker as if on a great throne, was by this time pouring up the Fraser Valley. It outlined every girder of Granville Bridge, until that normally ugly span became a magic and intricate web. It bathed a travelling bus in that same glow, changing the ordinary tired commuters into distant heads with golden crowns. As I came over the crest of the bridge, the sun ran between some highrise buildings so that they appeared as transparencies. The new Simpsons building, with its circular top and its central concrete spire, looked for a moment like an infinitely tall lady in a shimmering negligee and a vast and ridiculously extravagant hat.

Finally beyond were the mountains. They had moved during the night and could almost be touched. They looked windswept, washed, and put out to dry in that morning sun. Then suddenly I was in the city, and the golden fantasy was gone. As I parked by the cathedral, I thought of a poet long ago, William Wordsworth, who found himself early one morning on London Bridge, and he began a sonnet with these lines:

Earth has not anything to show more fair:
Dull would he be of soul who could pass by
A sight so touching in its majesty:
This city now doth like a garment wear
The beauty of the morning.

I parked my Mini, went into the cathedral, and celebrated the Eucharist, the holy "thanksgiving."

Kozmas

It was a family celebration, and to observe it we had gone out for supper (a decision, I might add, not casually taken these days).

Nowadays a restaurant is no longer merely a building. Restaurants have changed from being buildings to being places of atmosphere. After that they have begun to be places where a tiny artificial world is created from the moment you enter. Inside the door of this particular restaurant every effort had been made to give you the impression that you have just stepped from the west coast of Canada to Greece, from Vancouver to, shall we say, Nauplia.

What is it that is so appealing, I asked myself, about these artificial images? The images are not really that consistent. The sheepskin on the wall is of course timeless and speaks of ancient rural Greece. The tiles on the low roof built inside as decor speak probably of a later Byzantine Greece. The statue is a distant and mass-produced echo of the glorious work of classical Greece. But why is it all so attractive, not just to me but to so many of us in the western world?

I suspect it is because it sends along the blood, through the eye and ear and smell, a host of half-forgotten race memories. So much of the world outside this closed door, so much of all we are, is sprung from all that was once the greatness of Greece. In a strange way, although I am a child of a colder and more northern island, and my children are of a continent no Greek ever knew, we are all, in this contrived atmosphere, to a small extent at home.

West End

I always think it interesting how public relations people, magazine photographers, tourist board brochure writers, are all determined to create a stereotype of the West End in our city. It is the abode, one is led to think, only of the young, the beautiful, and the affluent. In reality, of course, it is the abode of an infinitely varied number of human beings who represent every age and every life style and every level of income.

There are people who can remember when a gentle green hill sloped up from Burrard Street and then fell away equally gently to the quiet bay. There are people who can remember when from behind curtains discreetly drawn came the sound of pianos as the songs of an Edwardian age, already slipping away, were played. There are people who remember when the ultimate romantic act was to have dinner in the Sylvia Hotel high above the sea and the city.

There are also people who never realize that all this was once real and loved. There are people who never realize that Stanley Park was once both wilder and, by a strange irony, safer than it is today. There are people who are so recently arrived that they still know only their own apartment block and a few necessary stores on Denman Street.

As I said, your West Ender can represent any age and any income level and any life style and any personal history. If only the image makers would realize it, this fact makes the mosaic of the West End infinitely more interesting than any image they may try to manufacture.

Long Beach

The road running along behind the beach is glistening with light rain. On either side the vegetation has that raw and ragged look that trees develop when they have weathered years of howling wind and blown salt spray.

Out of the car, on with an Anorack, down the soft brown pathway, over a last mound. One's eyes leap out and far away. Beyond the white tumble of logs on the higher beach, across the glistening grey sand, out to the first white line of foam, then across the endless heaving desert that rolls across the next quarter of the planet.

Immensity, calm, the breath of morning wind from the ocean, endless movement, yet eternal and vast stillness. Strange how it never loses its spell. I find myself thinking of lines which William Wordsworth wrote as he watched another ocean in another century.

> I have seen
> A curious child, who dwelt upon a tract
> Of inland ground, applying to his ear
> The convolutions of a smooth-lipped shell;
> To which in silence hushed, his very soul
> Listened intensely; and his countenance soon
> Brightened with joy; for from within were heard
> Murmurings, whereby the monitor expressed
> Mysterious union with its native sea.

So Wordsworth wrote, probably seeing in his mind's eye the wild and cold North Sea coast. Where I stood by this other ocean, the mist continued, drifting warmly past my face as we headed back for Wickininish and the distant wind-blown trees.

Similkameen

Even the very name is a thing of beauty. They call it Similkameen. What is that figure of speech when the sound of a word actually brings to mind the thing it names? I think it's onomatopoeia. Similkameen speaks of smoothness, of calm, of peace. And in a sense that is true.

I am standing on an earthen piece of road where it crosses the river. As I drove here, this river and I kept on catching each other's eye. At times it would chatter and twist among stones and fallen trees; suddenly it would lose me again and play hide and seek in a small valley, or behind a hill or among thick woods. When I had thought it gone, it would suddenly leap out to the highway's edge and run along beside me, then disappear under me, and later emerge on the other side only to be lost again.

Now at last we meet face to face, and I have a chance to hear its voice as well. I look back along the surface until it is lost in the trees. It comes to me from those trees, first over a bed of stones which break it and give it a thousand reflections, then through a stretch of calm. Always shallow, it lingers between the banks until it begins to gather for the plunge through the narrow opening underneath where I am standing. As it rushes toward me its voice grows. It sings and calls, and suddenly it is gone. When I turn it floods out on the other side into a wide shallow lake, which also begins leaping again among the next barrier of rocks. So it goes on and on to the south-east where I can no longer follow. The Similkameen, a thing of loveliness and endless variation . . .

Trans Canada

There is something we possess in Canada that we take totally for granted, yet it could be said to be one of the wonders of the world. The two reasons why we don't see it like that are, first, we are rather jaded with wonders to the point of losing the capacity to wonder and, second, it is almost impossible to imagine that it could be both Canadian and wonderful.

That thought occurred to me as I stood by a low wall at the side of the Trans Canada Highway. Behind me a steep mountain side rose. Before me stretched a huge lake; across the water the late afternoon sun spilled its sparkling golden warmth. And what is so wonderful? The highway is! That seemingly ordinary dark streak with its white dotted lines and its solid lines, its infinitely varied sign posts, its rest areas, its over-passes that hiss and roar, its multiple choices presented again and again for the choosing of your journey, its view points, its garbage gobblers, and its passing lanes.

The Trans Canada Highway can take me from the foyer of the Empress Hotel in Victoria to the top of Telegraph Hill in St John's, Newfoundland. It gives not a fig about the universes yawning politically between Calgary and Ottawa. It just links them like a wise and impatient parent getting two children to make up. It is a far greater achievement than John McDonald's railroad. It shows you the glory of Canada that no glamorous 747 aloft can ever do. It is a wonderful thing, this totally taken for granted Trans Canada Highway . . .

Squilax

The store once fronted onto the lakeshore road. Nowadays the road has become a highway. In fact it has become the great highway that we in this country take so much for granted. Yet, in that it twists and turns and travels from one coast to another, it is an amazing thing. But we must go back to the store.

It stands at the side of this highway. Across the other side is a steep hill that gives shade from the pitiless sun for part of the morning. The wood of the store front is dried and faded from that same sun.

Over the door is their name. At least it's his name, because when they put it up nobody had ever heard of things like marriage contracts or equal rights or liberation. Instead there were wierd things like vows and loyalty and "till death us do part." I say this because when you go in they are quite often both there. They move very slowly now, and all their prices are written in a book so that they can remember them. They have a little bit of a great number of things. They have biscuits in those large tins with glass tops, and they have some pots of local honey. When we questioned the modest price of a two pound jar of honey, she first of all looked it up again in the book and said, Yes, that was the price. She guessed that inflation hadn't caught up with that jar because they had had it in stock for quite a while. (I immediately thought of half a dozen large corporations who should consider this as a sales policy.)

They have been there now thirty-five years. Behind them the lake water really does (as Yeats once said) "lap with low sounds by the shore." It was a very rich discovery to push open their door and to meet them . . . .

The Canyon in Wintertime

I have lived a decade in this province, and I have always associated this particular journey with summer. First there is the valley, the fields stretching away to the south, and beyond them the as yet distant mountains. Mile after mile the mountains march nearer, until they and the great meandering river agree to let me take my ant-like journey through them. The climb then begins through the canyon, and beyond Lytton the first far vistas appear. Later, beyond Spence's Bridge, come the wide reaches of Walachin, full of the dreams of a long ago generation who tried but failed to make the great valley bloom.

It has always been summer for me here. Now, when I visit for the first time in winter, I notice how nature almost totally repossesses this wilderness. It is as if she relinquishes it to us for a few weeks and then, as the light shortens, she repossesses it. The human race is gone. There are traces of our summer existence, places we once were allowed to do our transient human busyness. Here is a stand announcing fresh fruit for our thirst and, incidentally, our gullibility. But now it is shuttered, and its windows gaze blindly through the fog. Here is a lookout, complete with historical message glistening and unread as the wind howls around it, beyond it the vistas hidden in the gathering darkness. Here below the highway and beside the river are the bare trees and snow covered areas of a campsite. But of the human race there is hardly a trace.

Oh yes, we are here. But, like me, the others are crouched over tightly held wheels, eyes carefully on the road. As we pass we glance at one another, seen dimly and grimly behind our partially frosted windows. We are strangers here, moving through a foreign land by permission of a ruler who wields his warriors of wind and weather, and gives us grudgingly our fleeting passage through his wild domain.

Foothills City

Strange, I had crossed no border, shown no passport, heard no change of language, yet there is a difference. I have come down over the mountains and moved across a vast green ocean of land. Gradually the city reaches out. It lets you know its presence long before you see it. Its outriders are the great trucks which are its screaming slaves. They rush to feed it and to stock it, they bring it spare parts and luxuries and furniture and gargantuan pieces of mysterious machinery and who knows what else.

The city is like a vast organism that opens its orifices to receive these supplies into its great glittering belly. It digests them while it sleeps and then distributes them, through its million concrete sinews and chrome veins and electronic nerve ends, to supply its insatiable need for energy, materials, power.

As you near the city, piercing its layers of suburban skin, you find that those great veins of highway are no longer sufficient for its life blood to flow. The city is already operating on itself in a score of places, anxiously and noisily widening its arteries, opening its veins with new highways and over-passes and by-passes, burrowing deep into its own vitals to put in rapid transit.

In the centre of it all beats its great heart. It is a new heart, and it has been created by oil. It glitters and shimmers under the summer skies, and sends its towers toward the sun. This city is at perpetual high noon. This is its hour. This is Calgary, Alberta, in a fleeting moment of geological time called the 1980s . . .

Alberta Morning

First there is the gravel driveway, then the hill falls away steeply in a long grassy slope browned by the Alberta sun. I look southwest across very gently rolling fields, countryside that is almost flat. I am high enough up to see the grid of country roads that roam over this area. From where I sit I can see a car leaving a trail of dust as it ambles in a leisurely way into the distance. The dust forms and then thins; as it fades it is wafted over the green fields and then dissipates into the blue sky.

Below me a field of black earth breaks the pattern of greens, as if the earth reserves the right tantalizingly to show the infinitely rich soil hidden under these grasses, flirting, coyly revealing its hidden beauty of growth and fertility.

Beyond these fields the woods begin, and there too begin the lands of the Sarcee Indian nation. Beyond the woods lie the nation's miles of rich land. There is nothing here, no sound, no machines, no towers topping the nearby ridge, to tell you that the edge of the city begins. If you look farther to the southwest, you see the end of the Sarcee lands. Your eye is on the first rising of the foothills. Beyond them a giant staircase begins to climb to the great hall of the mountain king, as old fairy stories would have put it. Finally, hidden in the heat haze of this Alberta day, the infinitely distant peaks rise, their stubborn snow patches like tiny detached wisps of clouds in a hazy sky. Such is this summer morning in southern Alberta . . .

Morning on the Prairie

The car had come only a few blocks for me; so it stood in the driveway, crouched against the snow banks, emitting great clouds of exhaust, as if unwilling to face this grey prairie dawn. I put the bag in the back and we moved through the as yet empty streets. At one intersection there was a flashing light, a huge power shovel and a group of heavily clad men gazing into a great black hole in the snowy street. At each red light the car crunched its way to a stop. To left and right the streets stretched away to a distant grey sky.

And then we were out on the highway, and on either side stretched the ocean of the endless land. Dotted across it the lights in early morning houses shone like the lights of little ships on a wide sea. And then the tall masted ships of this prairie ocean began to loom out of the fading shadows, the grain elevators marking the line of the unseen railway. Once upon a time the clippers sailed to China across another ocean. Now the grain in these great holds on this prairie goes once again to China.

On and on we go, the car undulating gently along the east bound ribbon of road, the surface made delicate and fluid by the endless weaving and drifting of light snow blown across it. We chat about this world in the middle of Canada. That plant over there, a long low dark gash against the snow, a log plant. Beyond it a line of hydro pylons march into the north-west. They stand cold, angular, steely, yet they carry power, warmth, light. They look like skeletons, yet they carry life itself. We move across this winter land in our cocoon of warm air, nylon padded seats, cheery voiced weather forecasting, and gas powered cylinders. Yet in this dawn we feel that we are as those who have been granted permission by a majestic and mighty emperor to move across this winter land, humble, fragile, transient.

Heritage Park

Among the amenities of every self-respecting modern city is a heritage park or village. City councils are proud of them. They are among the very few decisions that meet with general approval. They are the guilt offering that the modern city places on the altar of the past. They are peace in the midst of turmoil, innocence in the midst of sophistication, simplicity in the midst of complexity. They allow us to taste all the former pleasures and at the same time to hurry back to the latter problems. Yet do they?

I am sitting with my back to a tree in the front garden of a lovely turn-of-the-century home. I am looking out on a shaded street of green trees. Along it winds a wooden boardwalk. As the evening shadows fall, the street will be gently lit by gas lamps placed along it at intervals. Suddenly, if anything is sudden in this carefully created environment, a bus or street car of the early 1900s passes by. Except for my clothes, Edward VIII could be on the distant throne of a powerful England and I could be making funny jokes with friends about the Kaiser, or reminiscing about the South African war.

The temptation is to think that those long ago days were days of sunlit peace and innocence and simplicity. There are reasons why we think this. For some it is because those days are seen through the eyes of childhood. For others there is the conviction that the past is better. But in reality, if you could enter again into that long ago afternoon, you would find that those people in turn spoke longingly of another golden time, another past, a lost simplicity, a remembered innocence. And so it will be to the end of that trickster we call time.

Gatineau

The other day I had the afternoon free from a workshop in which I was involved in Ottawa. I had borrowed a car from friends and I headed out over the Ottawa River and up the Gatineau Parkway. It winds higher and higher into the hills north of the city. You pass small lakes with trails around them. There still appear the echoes of the glory of fall, even though this year the colours were muted. On and on you go, past the Mackenzie King estate, and finally you are at the lookout. You can see both north and west. Below you across the endless rolling countryside flows the Ottawa River. It comes down from the north before turning east to pass by the Houses of Parliament.

It was about four in the afternoon, and so the October sun was lowering and weakening. The world seemed enveloped in the blue smoky haze of late fall, turning to grey as the light died.

The greatness of the Ottawa river is easily forgotten because it flows into the vast St Lawrence. But this river is the symbol taken years ago by Hugh MacLennan to start off his classic Canadian book *Two Solitudes*. He spoke of the river as flowing between two solitudes, Ontario and Quebec. As I stood on this Quebec hill top and looked over the great wide valley below me, then across the river to Ontario beyond, I was very aware that the two solitudes now pose a much more threatening reality. I found myself silently wondering if it was possible that across this panorama, one land since the dawn of time, there would be a political frontier?

Gradually the sun sank lower. The air changed and I turned toward the car. As I drove down across the hills, the lights of Ottawa and Hull began to come on in the dusk . . .

Huron

It is very early on a Saturday morning as we drive through the still empty streets of Sarnia and head north along the coast road. We are moving through rich Ontario farm country, neat and ordered with the appearance of country peopled for a long time. At times, out to the west, the land falls away toward the lake. It is less a lake than an inland ocean. It is Lake Huron.

This morning, as October brings this countryside toward another winter, the lake is grey and misted. Over it, stretching as far from south to north as the eye can see, there is an endless bank of grey massed cloud holding the first snow that is to come. At a certain stage along this coast we arrive at the Conference Centre which is our destination.

Here the land is a little higher. You can see some miles north. As I look up along the coast, the first white curtain of sleet moves in from the grey water and comes in over the land. I wish I could drive farther, up where these fields disappear and the thin earth reveals the older rocks. I wish I could travel up the coast where it becomes more broken as you move along the Bruce Peninsula. Because up there they came a long time ago, now nearly half a century, and they looked at the harsh lonely glory of it all, and they wrestled to capture it on canvas. They succeeded and gave a younger Canada her own art and her own beauty. We call them the Group of Seven. They felt the same wind and saw the same white sleet from the lake that now sends my friend and me running for the house, bent against the wind.

Kingston

We take it for granted now that our capital city is where it is, that the great pillar of the Peace Tower stands above the Ottawa River. But it could so easily have been otherwise. Had Victoria and her advisors so decided, this country would be centred on these gracious quiet streets through which I am walking.

This afternoon the light is mellow and shadowed as October ends. The old trees that line the streets are still clinging to the last of their leaves. I have just asked my way of somebody, and they tell me to take a shortcut across the cricket pitch. It has been many years since white flannelled figures played in this far corner of empire. Now the area is a common surrounded by university buildings on one side and gracious old houses on the other.

The doorways are arched, the houses sometimes fronted with iron railings. Frequently the curtains are deliberately traditionally patterned. As I continue walking, getting the feel of the streets, it has now begun to rain, the evening light is failing, the sidewalks are beginning to glisten. I walk these streets from a surging and vigorous western Canada, a Canada that this city once upon a time saw only as empty, infinitely distant, unreal. As I walk, the lights begin to appear, the bells of a church peal the hour of six, and I come out underneath the dome of the old cathedral, feeling in my bones a long story which, please God, is far from ended.

Shoreline

I am heading out under an archway. It is built of stone and two great heavy wooden doors hang in it. Nowadays they are always open. I walk out through them and head down the now surfaced driveway. Once the gravel crunched and scattered under horses' hoofs and carriage wheels. This is Kingston, Ontario.

I move out under the gate and across the nearby street, then on down the gentle slope heading south to the lake. I wonder if I can get to it and back before the next lecture I am due to give at the university. A few blocks, across another broad street, and by the entrance of a large granite building housing the Solicitor General's office. The grounds are well kept. I pass the house and walk toward the edge of the river, which here is wide enough to be a lake. The water has a grey-black look that warns of winter. It laps gently below me. Across the river I can see the American shoreline. To my right and away over to the west there is a distant tiny island with a few scattered trees. It is far enough away to appear to resemble an eighteenth-century four-master lying out in midstream. If I look toward the east, I can see the promontory on which Fort Henry stands, its guns resting after the tourist season, eager to thunder as entertainment because they never thundered toward that opposite shore as they were built to do. I am aware of being the richer for feeling in my bones this long ago story.

Between Two Worlds

The wide platform is bathed in sunlight. Away from me to left and right the gleaming tracks run as far as my eye can see. I am looking down them for a purpose. Behind me, splashed in the cloud and pale sunshine of late fall, is the old city of Kingston.

Far down the track there is movement, a distant image. It slowly assumes a shape, and then with sudden swiftness grows. Its vibrations shake the ground I stand on as it rumbles by me, vast and leisured, moving with immense dignity. A voice announces its arrival. It is inconceivable that something so fine as this should arrive anywhere without being announced, and in two languages! I realize again how easy it is on our far western coast to forget this other reality, this duality which is everywhere here. The train I climb aboard is a satellite moving between two worlds. This morning it moved past the great cross on Mount Royal, glided out into the countryside by a silver church spire of Quebec, rumbled across the Ottawa River bridges, and entered Ontario. This evening it will nose its way through the outer reaches of Toronto, and come to a halt in the shadow of another kind of world that possesses another kind of story and has the security of its own history. In the cars are mingled copies of *Le Devoir* and the *Globe and Mail*. This great train has crossed no frontier, entered no customs barrier, yet it moves between two worlds. Should the two worlds remain one, we all in this country will be the richer.

Berwick

I sometimes wonder if the fundamental difference between us and our fathers is that we are inveterate doubters. We look, we see something, and we do not presume that what appears to us is the reality. We see a thing and we tend to presume that the reality is different. We are Freudian through and through, looking for the underbelly of life, the shadow under the sunlight, the deception under the promise, the storm behind the stillness.

Look at this village. I have lived on its edge now for a few days. It has been here in this valley since the late eighteenth century. They cleared the woods, and the soldiers cut the rough track to connect the fort at Halifax with the ships on the Bay of Fundy.

On the surface the town is utterly peaceful. There are gardens with a child's swing. There are white-painted windows swept by green branches in a golden sunset. There is a main street that is ready to allow you to walk slowly or to cross it, even if you are very old or indeed very young. There are a few shops, a few cars parked, a smell of freshly baked bread in the air.

But my doubting mind wants to question the stillness. And if you do look carefully, you see another reality. Things that seemed far removed are here. They are slightly hidden but they are still there. From a car there comes the frantic false macho voice of a disc jockey. There are television antennae above the white clapboards. There are the applications for Master Charge and Visa on the restaurant counters, and out beyond the rise at the end of the leafy street is the highway sullenly roaring and snarling. Behind this seeming peace is all the pressure, all the anxiety, all the carefully orchestrated discontent of our larger society. Because part of the humour and agony of us all is that we seek both peace and discontent.

Valley Road

I borrowed a time machine and drove it into the eighteenth century today. The land I passed through was a valley between the sea and the forest. The faces I saw were those of people who came to this lovely valley before the road, before the fields, before the orchards that nowadays make the air heavy and sweet with the scent of the yearly apple blossom.

Perhaps the very words *apple blossom* will give you a clue to where I was. My time machine was a Honda Civic lent by a friend, and the miles I drove took me down through one of the loveliest areas of Canada, the Annapolis Valley in western Nova Scotia.

For many years the road I drove on was the only road. It is now the "old road" because, as you can guess, a new super highway sweeps you from Halifax to Yarmouth. It puts you on the ferry having ensured that you have seen nothing. But the old road is the way of the little towns which have grown here over two and a half centuries. They were first laid down as forest clearings and then as military outposts and finally as towns. The old road is the way of country fruit stands with their bottles of cider and their jars of honey, yellow and golden in the sun, surrounded by the greens and browns of fresh vegetables taken from the fields that stretch on either side of the road.

There was a time when this road did not exist in this valley. First there was a track through the forest. Unbelievably it crossed the province from the fort at Halifax nearly a hundred miles away, and down it solitary messengers frequently trudged or rode. Then there came the thunder of horses' hoofs and after them the grinding of coaches' wheels. And far on in this human procession I come, guiding my little time machine and feeling history everywhere.

Fundy

I am still on what was for me a fascinating day driving down the Annapolis Valley in Nova Scotia. I had only a few hours between the morning and evening sessions of a conference.

About three o'clock or so the sky clouded over and the scenery changed. I was now at the southwestern end of the valley, quickly nearing the arm of water that eventually opens out into a huge bay. Just as I reached the end of the arm a light mist began, and the moored fishing boats began to lift and strain as the water became choppy. Beyond them I could see the coast as it swept around this water, curving until two great headlands framed the opening out to the Bay of Fundy and then to the Atlantic itself.

Perhaps it was because I had just come from the west coast, and the sight of some tall masted sailing ships visiting Vancouver was still fresh in my mind. But I couldn't help thinking of masts and sails on this water nearly two centuries before James Cook rounded the headland into Nootka Sound on faraway Vancouver Island. It was the year 1605, and in through that opening which I could see in the grey distance came two ships, to our eyes pitiably small, their sails torn, their ship's company exhausted and depressed. Those were the ships of Samuel de Champlain and Sieur de Monts. They sailed up this inland water, and on its northern shore they erected their habitation at what is today Port Royal. They didn't realize it, but they were beginning a new chapter, a new world in the human story.

When you look across the grey water, you get a measure of the loneliness and vulnerability of that long ago community as you realize that the nearest European settlement in the western hemisphere was then as far away as Mexico. It was fascinating to stand and look at history.

The Fleeing Acadians

I am standing at the intersection of a two laned surfaced road and a gravelled country road that winds away westward until it is lost in the trees still covering the slope of the valley. The name of the valley is Annapolis and it holds a great part of the history of this country. And the immediate area I'm standing in holds a particularly poignant chapter of that history.

At this crossroads I am facing west. I am standing at the corner of the large immaculately kept graveyard in which stands the Church of St Mary. Look beyond the church to the other slope of the valley. Beyond that low ridge is the shore of the Bay of Fundy. A long time ago this shore witnessed human agony. In 1755, hearing that they were about to be expelled from Annapolis, 300 Acadians tried to reach French soil in what is now New Brunswick. They reached this area. It was getting late into autumn. They didn't realize, but winter was to be early that year.

They made a camp, erected whatever crude shelters they could, and tried to ride out the winter. After a while their gun powder and ammunition gave out, and that meant an end to hunting. One source of food remained. By chance the shore was alive with mussels, clinging to the rocks at low tide. These they desperately gathered day by day, tide by tide. As the agony of exposure got worse, the Acadians began to die. By the time spring came, only a handful were left to make the crossing of the Bay of Fundy.

Green Gables

Shrines are extraordinary places. Sometimes in older societies they have evolved over many centuries. There is an event recalled, a battle, a place of ancient worship or even more ancient superstition. There is sometimes an association with a saintly life. Such are the shrines of an old world.

But we Canadians have few such shrines. The years have not yet added up to make them. We have others. Sometimes they are places where nature has fashioned a wonderful thing that fills us with awe, a Niagara Falls or a Nahanni River gorge. Like all shrines we vulgarize them if enough of us can get to them. But so does Europe — and everywhere else.

Here on this rainy hillside in Prince Edward Island is another kind of shrine. It is neither ancient nor of a saint nor mysterious. Yet it brings people from all over the world and, maybe most surprising of all, from Japan, where children know this hill, the fields surrounding it, the nineteenth century farmhouse, as a place very familiar to them, even though it is in a culture very unlike their own.

I'm referring of course to Green Gables and its heroine named Anne, who was made immortal by Lucy Maud Montgomery and has travelled in translation all over the world. When you move through the house, all is so banal and ordinary that you cannot but ask why the legend exists, why this shrine attracts so many people. Here is Anne's kitchen, Anne's bedroom; here is this and that and on and on, until you are once again at the door and you are wondering why and how it all evolved. You look at the fields, the rolling hills, the distant sea, the road winding away to other hamlets and farms, and you realize that what is being venerated here at Green Gables is innocence. People come here to find the lost garden of their own childhood, a remembered arcadia where afternoons were endless and the fields smelled sweet, a time out of time when love and peace and plenty reigned supreme. People come here to discover a lost dream.

Confederation House

The first thing you notice is the flagstone just in front of the main door. It is smooth and hollowed out from the countless feet that have stepped through here in the last one hundred and thirty-five years.

You enter a high Georgian hallway, the stairs ascending on each side of the space in front of you. The building is almost completely silent except for sounds from the street outside. On the first floor hallway a commissionaire stands. Beyond him, to one end of the building, a double door opens to reveal the heavy wood of the speaker's chair and the table bearing the mace. Obviously that is the legislative chamber, significant because it is one of the oldest such chambers in the country. To my left, its counterpart at the other end of the long corridor, is the room I have come to see. We walk toward it and stop by the low wooden railing which contains the visitors who are always entering this room.

What dominates is the huge table. It sits here in its never ending retirement, silently witnessing to the event that took place on that long ago day. The chairs stand around it mute and empty. In front of each chair is a name on a brass plaque on the table. Behind on the wall hangs the huge picture showing the events of that day. The names are carefully attached to the men who stand around in studied Victorian casualness, names such as Tupper, D'Arcy Magee, Cartier, MacDonald. It was September when they came to this lovely rural island, once called St John's Isle and later Prince Edward Island. In this room they brought to birth something we call Confederation. It was not completed here that day, but it was begun.

We left the room and walked to the other end of the hall to look at the legislative chamber. We went down the stairs and out into the November sunlight. I thought of the struggle going on for the continued life of what began here, a fragile life called Canada.

Yesterdays

Sharing one's own memories can be a tricky business. After all, something remembered can be infinitely rich to oneself and yet of no interest to others whatsoever. Yet there is also a way to share memories which can be rich for oneself and others, precisely because the experience shared is universal.

Forbidden Fruit

For reasons which we shall refer to merely as patterns of our family life, I find myself with reasonable frequency in the warm and carefully coloured world of MacDonalds. Recently it came to pass that I emerged from the said establishment having purchased, for our twelve year old, what is called in contemporary parlance a "large fries."

But for some reason I stepped into a kind of time change. I think it happened because I was suddenly struck by the ease and casualness with which my offspring could buy a "fries," and how very difficult it was for me at that stage.

For me, in a city far away and long ago, French fries (or chips) were for some mysterious middle class reason out of bounds. Funnily enough, it was acceptable to eat chips in a restaurant. But to visit a chip shop was, if I may use an expression, quite a different kettle of fish. The chip shop (I knew of no other) was down a narrow and dark street. It was dimly lit, as if the proprietor realized that his trade was somehow improper. The floor was covered with saw dust. On the counter was a pile of newspapers. Every inch of the grubby glass window was steamed up. The man himself was a happy go lucky jocular type who seemed not a bit ashamed of his (heaven help us) low class trade. In fact, he seemed to revel in it. He dug into the great bubbling oil, shook the basket, dollopped out the contents, wrapped the paper around them with a flourish, and handed them to you. There you were, once more out in the dark side street, your fingers shiny, your mouth full, and of course, your whole being borne up with the heady joy of having been where you were not supposed to be.

I realize that what is missing from the taste of today's French fries is simply this — they lack the delicious flavour of forbidden fruit . . .

Messiah

A word suddenly jumped out of a half-listened to radio program, the word *Dublin*. This year, the voice was saying, such and such a choir are going to sing the Dublin version of *The Messiah*.

For a moment come for a walk. If you ever get a chance to take this journey in actuality then do take it, because it's worth it. Let me tell you how and when I used to take it. You may go by taxi, but if the year is 1950 and you are a student, you will probably catch a double decker bus outside Trinity College and watch the December streets, as you move toward the heart of the city across the widest city bridge in Europe. From there you turn west along the quays passing the isolated magnificence of the Four Courts.

When you leave the bus, you start walking into a warren of small streets, dimly lit as evening comes. Eventually you come to the grime blackened church of St Michan. It lies in an area of Dublin south of and across the river from the old Norse city. I used to go there very often because a fellow student's brother was the priest there, and the food was good, and there were first class table tennis tables.

One December evening as we played, there came from the church the sound of singing. We put our heads in. The choir was getting ready a section of *The Messiah*. As they did, we found it fascinating to look around the dimly lit church, to realize that it was on that small organ high up in the balcony that Mr Handel had once played, that in these pews sat those who had come long ago on an evening such as this to hear Mr Handel's music called *The Messiah*.

I found myself wondering if, as they emerged long ago into these same streets, climbing into their carriages to be taken back to their warm Georgian houses, they realized that they were the first to hear what may yet be heard by countless generations . . .

Barley Sugar

What a complex and fascinating number of layers lie within each of us. This is a simple thing but I tell it to you because it will trigger other thoughts in you. I had to go to Edmonton for a few hours, but before I boarded the plane I bought some barley sugar. I don't know why. Why does one do a thousand small things. I just did. And soon I was seated in the cabin, listening to its many sounds, of whirring ventilators, announcements, clicking seat belts, the whine of engines. Beyond the windows the coast range shimmered in a day of west coast Indian summer. So I opened a piece of barley sugar and found, as one so often does, that there is magic in simple things. As I tasted it, everything changed. The great plane, the background music, the distant mountains, all vanished. In their place was something totally different.

I was seated on a folded sack on a wooden seat in a small cart. In my hands, very small hands, the hands of an eight or nine year old boy, were the worn leather reins that went forward to the harness of a large brown donkey who pulled us along. Beside me on the seat was my grandfather. Behind us, swaying and rattling a little, were the churns in which we were taking the days milk from the farm to the creamery. About a mile and a half away, down this quiet winding earthen road, would be the town. In the town, when our chores were done, my grandfather would tie up the donkey in some suitable spot, and he and I would go to the newsagents for a paper. There beside the papers would be a jar. It was a gargantuan jar. Within it stood great golden pillars. Could they have been a foot long? I doubt it now, but they certainly seemed so then! They were twisted gold. And a stick of that barley sugar would be mine. All the way home I would enjoy it, through the town and up the hill and past the green fields and the little lake, until the chimney of the farm house would appear beyond the hill and the donkey would begin to trot because he knew the journey's end was near.

But the wooden seat has changed again. And someone is asking me to fasten my seatbelt for another journey across mountains I now call home.

Change and Decay

We are becoming adept at creating atmospheres in which we eat. There was a time when you merely ate in a restaurant or a hotel dining room. There were always plants in such places and a high proportion of cane-seated chairs. There were waitresses with little white fronts and hats, and over it all there hung a certain air of solemnity.

I remember when I was a child a restaurant visit was a very special experience. My earliest recollection as a small child is of a strange world stretching into the distance, a kind of Cathedral whose roof was linen cloths and whose pillars were the legs and lower torsos of countless people. There I crouched, between two and three years of age I would surmise, on the gleaming hardwood floor of the dining room of the International Hotel in Killarney, eyeball to eyeball with an understanding waiter who had descended to see how I was getting on.

It has just struck me that, however solemn waiters were in that long ago world and however swinging the world of today is, it would be hard to find a waiter in this fair city (especially in one of its exclusive and sophisticated eateries) willing to stoop low, literally and metaphorically, to accommodate a child. I thought of him not long ago as I entered the same International Hotel in Killarney, this time with children of my own, grown however beyond the stage of crawling under tables. Alas, what a drab and limited world it had become. In place of my father's glorious and noble model T Ford in the driveway, there were seven huge tour buses in a parking lot, their fumes steadily poisoning some jaded looking nags standing listlessly between the shafts of their ancient jaunting cars. In the restaurant there were booths with plastic seats and washable table tops. In the land that had received the sacred potato from Sir Walter Raleigh himself, the French-fried variety reigned supreme, and if any child did have the wish to explore the floor, I am quite sure that not one of the bored youths who threw our food at us would have glanced at him or her. You see, though I am a gentle fellow, I must be allowed my bit of spleen sometimes!

Circus

I can remember the first time I ever saw a circus. I recalled it recently when one day I took our two youngest to a sad and shabby thing that presumed to be known by the ancient and respected word *circus*. We sat in the great clammy vault of the Agrodome and looked far down to two distant rings where weary elephants, a bored brace of tigers, and some other assorted creatures shuffled and tottered through their uninspired routines. The human beings addressed us through thundering microphones whose heavy black cables punctured all the pitiable illusions of forest or strange land, reducing lion tamers, fire eaters, trapeze artists to the most ordinary of mortals.

I can recall my first circus. I am a small boy in a long line of boys. In front are the smallest, at the back are the oldest. I am somewhere in between. We are moving through the village street at the end of the school driveway. We are now outside the village, and there in the field is the great tent. The wind is whipping the countless tiny flags that adorn the tent, and beyond them the wind is driving the myriad tiny clouds in a September blue sky. High up on a podium there is a band, and suddenly we see a senior school boy who is now strangely transformed into a daring horseback rider. This is his father's circus and one day will be his. Indeed, as I write at this moment, it still is. There is a warmth and a noise and a liveliness and an immediacy to it all.

Yet, as you yourself must sometimes do, I wonder. Were the elephants in that circus really any bigger? were those long ago lions any more noble? was the lady on the trapeze more beautiful? Maybe not. Circuses need to be seen by a child's eye undimmed and unjaundiced by adult doubt. But I am afraid I am stubborn. I still think that I got a far greater thrill from my long ago circus than my children got from this one.

Dooley's Lorry

A child has a passionate determination to make the ordinary into the exotic and romantic. In fact, for a child there is no ordinary. So much remains unknown and unfamiliar that the whole experience is full of wonder. I find the memory of all this always waiting to be touched and revived.

One day recently it sat outside the new offices on Hornby Street, gleaming, high, straight, different. The coach work was perfect, the great head lights shone, the wheel spokes were thick and strong and solid. And for some reason, when I saw it, I was reminded again of Dooley's Lorry.

Nowadays it would be called a truck, but then a small child called such things lorries. Dooley used to park it in the farm-yard and leave it all day. My father told me years later that Dooley worked in the town but, since he could not afford the price of a licence for his vehicle, he left it here with my grand-father's permission. Every morning by a kind of magic it would be there. It never came, if you understand, it was just mysteriously and magnificently there. It was an open-topped model of heaven knows what vintage. The tires were solid, the steering wheel was immense and massive, the seat leather was ancient and shiny and wrinkled and smelled of many things, among them tobacco, petrol, and oil. As a child I would stand on the running board and climb over the door to sit in the driver's seat. In a child's mind the great engine would cough into life, the panels of the bonnet or hood would vibrate, and I would travel across hills and fields and counties until voices called me back to the demands and duties of the so-called real world.

In the evening Dooley himself would appear. He would climb up where I had been, and the engine would in truth cough and shudder into thundering life. The great wheels would move, and Dooley would wave to me, and I to him, as he drove down the driveway and out of the gates. I would stand and wave until the sound of him had died on the scented evening air.

Appearances

How wrong we can be in our easy assessment of people. Sometimes, if we are fortunate, the transient encounter where we make a wrong assessment can grow into a continuing relationship where we have an opportunity to correct our mistake. Nobody makes quicker mutual assessments than the young, and since compassion is on the whole the gift of later years, some youthful assessing of others can be brutal.

I have a figure in mind, a master in a boarding school. This memory is from that benighted and primitive age when teachers were called masters and mistresses. He was the butt of many jokes. Physically, he was a weakling. He had a sunken chest, pidgeon toes, little height, a squeaky voice, and as if that wasn't enough, crossed eyes.

He came into a school where the four main religions were rugby, hockey, tennis, and cricket. His first year must have been agony. Yet little by little something happened. In spite of our teenaged savagery we became aware of somebody who had a mind like the proverbial steel trap, a real gift for teaching, and a delicious sense of humour. I shall always remember his great moment.

It was the afternoon of a summer day, the last class before freedom. Beyond the window of the Sixth Form, the school orchard stretched away to the edge of the cricket pitch. The subject was Virgil's *Aeneid*. Suddenly the doors swung open and in shambled the school donkey. Somehow he had left the yard and come wandering indoors. Then, as the animal and the class looked at each other in mutual disbelief, before there was the inevitable chasing from the premises, Mr Jones (that is not his real name) was heard to quote scripture. "He came unto his own," he said quietly, "and his own received him not."

I often recall this memory when outward appearance tempts me to make judgements.

Favourite Uncles

Because I was given for Christmas a photo album, I was bestirred to tackle the immense number of photographs that lie in boxes in dusty corners. This is actually a fearful task. Going through photographs is like looking up a subject in the Britannica or in some other fascinating reference. You not only look up the first thing, but you start reading what comes before it and what comes after it, and that leads to another, and so on without end.

I want to show you a photograph. It is an old photograph of my favourite uncle. Everyone has a favourite uncle, and if they haven't, they should. Mine was (and indeed still is) my mother's youngest brother. If not already a romantic figure by the fact that he could ride both a horse and a motor bike, he was even more romantic by the fact that he had gone to the United States and Canada. There he had stayed with a relative from an even earlier generation who had owned a farm in western Canada. Here he is grinning happily, his face bronzed and handsome. He is clad in open shirt and some sort of leggings, a wide brimmed hat hanging from one hand. He sits on the front wheel of a great tractor at the edge of a vast wheat field.

Was ever the dream of a small boy so vindicated as mine was by that photograph? Dream and reality became one. All that was needed was for me to mount myself into the great throbbing driving seat of that tractor, grasp its quivering wheel in my brawny arms, and take it thundering and lurching out across the great golden sea of endless wheat.

Messages

Each of us swims in a great ocean of media. Television programs, radio music, newspapers, advertising hoardings, public relationship campaigns. The great tide never ends. I notice that my family call advertisements on television "messages." This seems to me to accord them unwarranted significance. But as I too am swept along by this great frothy tide, I reserve my own opinions about it all.

Sex

I was reading the newspaper version of a new report. It was about the problems that so many people have today in getting to sleep. The doctors who compiled the report were warning against the easy way some of us use sleeping pills. They then went on to suggest various other aids to sound sleep. One way was to take a walk before going to bed. Somewhere in the list they suggested what they called "sex."

Well, you say, what's wrong with that? There is nothing wrong with it, but there is something wrong and sad about the use of that short stark little word. I can remember some years ago a certain lady member of the House of Parliament in British Columbia sending the house into stitches with the serious plea to outlaw the word *sex* and to find another word. To say that one of the ways you can get to sleep is to *use* a *thing* called "sex" is to reduce something infinitely complex, deep, and profound to a pitiable banality. It's rather like saying that the Mona Lisa, the Sistine Chapel, and a Van Gogh are a *thing* called "paint," that Beethoven's Ninth Symphony, Brahms' Lullaby, and Bernstein's Mass are a *thing* called "noise." Of course they are noise, but they are very much more. They are infinitely and inexpressably more. What takes place between two human beings is infinitely more than a thing or a device for inducing sleep. Put that way, sex sounds like something you could buy at a $1.49 Day Sale, batteries not included.

If we are going to refer to one of the basic elements of existence, one of the facets of life that has exhausted most poetry and art to express it, let's at least refer to it as sexual intercourse (pointing to its involving human dialogue), or let's use that ageless if not hip term "making love," but above all let's not relegate it to a dreary list of sleep inducing devices such as Sominex, Valium, and sheep-counting!

Mork

For me the circus has never lost its attraction, especially the clowns. As children we laugh at clowns. Later, as adults, we laugh again. But then we become aware of another perception: that the fall of the clown is our fall, that he is acting out the loser in all of us, and that when he runs away from the ring, he is everything in us that makes us want to run away and hide.

There is a new clown among us, this time not in the familiar dusty circus ring but in a far greater arena, that of television. Those who watch him are in the millions, yet his attraction is as old as the medieval jester. His name is Mork, and the program is called *Mork and Mindy*. Nobody says that Mork is a clown. He is an extraterrestrial visitor. But in reality he is a clown with all the clown's deceptive mingling of foolishness and wisdom, fear and trust, laughter and tears.

Watch *Mork and Mindy* sometime. Watch it with your children if you have children. If your children are no longer at home, or if you do not have them, watch it with the child that is hidden inside yourself. Notice certain things about it. Notice how Mork is a kind of innocent because he is among us earthlings but yet is not one of us. Still, his innocence is seen to be the deepest wisdom. Notice how Mork is supposed to have no emotions, yet everything about him belies this and reveals tenderness, fear, anxiety, and vulnerability. This is a kind of parable of contemporary humanity. Finally, notice how at the end of each program Mork has a reference point, a voice, a presence, someone with whom he can reflect on the action and relationships he has experienced that day. Does that remind you, admittedly, obliquely, and in the disguise of humour, of something most of us have lost — the faith that there exists one who is aware of us, who listens to our longing for meaning, and who is the God to whom we can pray.

Farrah and Cheryl

A few weeks ago there was some excitement in our house, at least in one section of our family. An event of considerable significance was about to take place. Warnings, or as we would say these days, publicity had been seen and noticed. Now the event was at hand. What kind of event was it? Well, it was of such significance that one of the most widely sold publications in our society gave it the ultimate prominence of cover face and story.

But enough. What, you say, is the event that would carry such significance? My answer is that the event was nothing less than the death and resurrection of a god. But, you say, how could that be? Surely such a thing would be the ultimate headline. And I reply that it did make most front pages as befits such an event.

I must stop tantalizing you. Neither am I being sacreligious. The element of the absurd in what I am saying is that of course the event is not called the death and rising of a god, neither is it seen as religious. Psychologically, however, it contains an element of both.

In a sentence, then, here is what has happened. This year Farrah Fawcett Majors left the cast of *Charlie's Angels* and was replaced (the same word you use for spark plugs or TV modular components) by Cheryl Ladd.

Farrah has now been seen on a million posters and is obviously a Venus figure. She is what the ancients meant by the concept of Venus. The ancients did not have posters; they had statues. When you see Cheryl Ladd, you can see that she is selected, not to be herself, but to be a succeeding personification of a concept stretching in a long line back through the centuries. The watcher can transfer his or her devotion easily. The succession is guaranteed. The god has died, or shall we say the god's contract has somehow changed or ended. So naturally, since the cult must go on, because like all cults it is extremely lucrative, the god must be brought to life again. We think we are so scientific and technical and totally modern. Up on Mount Olympus the gods must be killing themselves with laughter.

Adult

Long ago, back in the 1930s, George Orwell wrote *1984*. In it he said that one of the marks of the future would be the way that language would be warped and twisted. In fact, Orwell said that words would be used to mean the very opposite of the thing they were describing. There would be, he said, a Ministry of Peace that would wage perpetual war, a Ministry of Truth that would perpetuate continual lies.

I thought of Orwell the other day when I was looking at the holiday season's entertainment page in the local newspaper. I found myself reading words on the movie page such as *adult* and *mature*. The words of course are put as labels on the various shows. I notice now that we are even developing variations. We now have entertainment that is "very adult" and "very mature."

The supreme irony of course is that in most cases the entertainment labelled "adult" and "mature," not to mention that most impressive adjective *very*, is in fact, both in its content and presentation, at the very opposite end of the spectrum from either adulthood or maturity. Since the world began, people have watched with fascination while somebody else more beautiful took off their clothes. Let's call it, shall we say, natural, but let's not call it adult or mature. It is natural to think in terms of bodies; it is mature to think in terms of persons. It is natural to watch an actor pulverize another human being with blows or shatter him with bullets, but it is not mature.

Actually, if we were true to language, we would advertise the symphony, the public library, the planetarium, and a film like *The Lord of the Rings* as "mature." After all, to pursue the beauty and terror and mystery and whimsy of life is truly mature. On the other hand, for *The Secrets of Eve* or *Call Girls in Outer Mongolia* and the eternal variations and permutations of *What the Butler Saw*, we should have helpful guide words like *sleazy*, *infantile*, perhaps indeed *immature*, and as a last resort, *very immature*.

God at the Movies

If anyone had said ten years ago that the films enjoying very lengthy runs in theatres nowadays would be religious, they would have been laughed at. In the late sixties we were moving through a period of debunking. The person who was getting debunked most was God. Prayer was regarded as a pathetic and meaningless thing. Faith, mysticism, spirituality were outmoded and relegated almost to being superstitions, worn out figments of the human imagination. God was dead.

Yet it is interesting to see precisely how today's films can be called religious. In other decades a religious film was religious in very definite and narrow terms. It was about something obviously religious. It was invariably solemn, larger than life, and very often wooden in its acting. Some such films were titled *The Ten Commandments*, *The Robe*, *Quo Vadis*, and *Ben Hur*. Sometimes they were redeemed a little, as in the case of *Barrabas*, by having the script written by a poet such as Christopher Fry.

Today we have movies like *Close Encounters of the Third Kind* and *Oh God*, and there is no doubt that they are religious films, in the sense that they express (though very contrastingly) elements of the deep and almost desperate search that contemporary man is engaged in. The reason for this search is that almost every issue facing us today forces us into the contemplation of the mystery of existence. In the new sciences such as genetics, in wrestling with our needs and the effects we have on our environment to fulfil those needs, in questions posed by body transplants, in agonies about abortion, in the technologies we now have for preserving life — in all these things we have opened possibilities for life and death. Most significantly, from the awe we feel before these things comes the return of an undirected and almost inarticulate but very real spirituality.

Sasquatch

The Monday morning newspaper. It is a day when one needs something special. There it is, every single ingredient one could have wished for. Taller than man. Emerging suddenly from the bush. Flared nostrils. Heaving chest. Afterward some puny human beings come and measure his footprint and his stride. Everything is as it should be with a good respectable Sasquatch or Bigfoot sighting.

However, having put it like that, let's not joke too much. It looks as if it was a genuine sighting. Maybe we will never know. I am prepared to accept the possibility that some such creatures exist, that it wasn't, for instance, a bear. But if so, perhaps the Sasquatch has a very important function. He, she, it provides us with something we need very badly to keep a sense of mystery. So above all, I think it most important that two things happen. First, that the Sasquatch show themselves at long and tantalizing intervals for short and tantalizing moments. Secondly, that if there are cameras the Sasquatch be just sufficiently hidden or far away as to remain again a tantalizing outline, no more. Thirdly and above all, the Sasquatch must never be captured. To think of a Sasquatch being thrown handfuls of croutons or nuts in the zoo in Stanley Park is not attractive.

We need monsters out there in the hills. We need them to be normal healthy monsters who feel hunger and desire and pain as we do, who feel the heat of the sun and who drink from running streams. In fact, we need them very badly, because if we do not have them we create far less healthy monsters within ourselves and our imaginations. The Sasquatch, whatever its history zoologically, is a thousand times more wholesome than endless paperbacks about the Bermuda triangle and endless expensive movies about children possessed by the devil.

Water Myth

Somebody in our house was reading an early James Bond book by Ian Fleming. We were talking about the Bond books and the movies which came from them. Somebody pointed out how, time and time again, Bond's life and death adventures are played out in the sea or in water.

How often Bond is found in the following kind of predicament! He is in the area of some undersea reef or cave, or in a great pool or a lagoon. He is in some way either near to, or surrounded by, enemies. They may be human enemies or creatures such as maneating fish. Fleming was fond of both piranha and sharks as symbols of terror. Always Bond will find an escape route, either a hidden cavern in the sea or a duct leading from the pool. Down it he will go, sometimes discovering even more danger down that passage in the shape of some terrible guardian or some almost insurmountable object. Suddenly he sees light; he shoots to the opening and finds himself on a ledge. From here he dives into the shimmering sea, and a waiting boat or ship picks him up.

We think it all so modern and contemporary. Yet it is the millionth retelling of the oldest myth in the world. The reason why we never tire of this tale is the simple but elemental reason that it is a journey we have all taken. We have all been prisoner in the waters of the womb. We have all been vulnerable to the dangers of that prenatal world. We have all found that long dark narrow passage where enemies of pain and terror and pressure have pursued us, and we have all struggled toward the light and emerged to those waiting for us. For the story is the story of our birth. Myths are everywhere, and they have endless fascination.

Mr Hua

The western press has been mightily impressed with the latest visitor from China, Mr (or rather President) Hua Kuo-Feng. The papers have been enthusiastic about his visit to eastern Europe. Features of everyday life, which in any one leader's daily doings would not get a line, are in Mr Hua's case being analysed for meaning. Soon, it is said, this visitor will come even to western Europe and walk the streets of Paris and possibly Brussels.

Things Chinese, at least mainland Chinese, intrigue the press still. There is about it the priceless touch of the exotic that is the lifeblood of media. It is presumed that things in that vast and distant kingdom cannot be pedestrian and ordinary, as they are here in our lesser kingdoms. In a way this is a kind of subtle and unconscious racism allowing one to deem the other person essentially different from one's self.

We have always, especially in popular literature, tended to do this to Asia. We have been brought up on phrases like "the inscrutable East." It was amusing to see the newspaper report recently, "Every move, every statement of Mr Hua, every toast and flowing wave of his carefully manicured hands has been carefully thought out." It seems that every detail of his lifestyle is examined for a reason. His hair used to be grey and now it is dyed black. Why? Is it unthinkable that it should be good old-fashioned vanity? He didn't smoke; now he does. Of course, it couldn't be ordinary weakness like yours or mine.

I am reminded of a beautiful story of Count Metternich in the nineteenth century who, when he was told that the Russian delegate to the Council of Europe had died just before its first session, remarked, "I wonder why he did that." We are a strange and funny lot, we humans.

WKRP Cincinnati

There are not many television programs that I see regularly. Now and again I find myself looking at pieces of two programs that are very much watched by other members of the household. One of these programs is *M*A*S*H* and the other is *WKRP Cincinnati*.

I don't imagine I have to tell you a great deal about either program. However, just in case you see even less television than I do, *M*A*S*H* and *WKRP* are both about groups of men and women who share a common experience that forces them to know each other very intimately for a long period of time. The setting of *M*A*S*H* is that of a medical unit in a war. *WKRP* is a radio station in a large American city.

When you watch either of these programs, and both of them have a very large following, you realize that what is being communicated is the cost of making human community possible, whether that group of people lives together, works together, studies together, or creates something together. The cost involves such things as an acceptance of one another's humanity, a knowledge, unavoidable after a while, of each other's limitations and vulnerabilities. Above all perhaps, it shows the need for the charity to accept those limitations in each other and to honour them. It also shows the need for a considerable supply of a sense of humour and a large helping of mutual trust. You might think me naive, but the mixture is suspiciously like a word the Bible uses a great deal, the word *charity* or *love*.

Gifts

Field Marshall Wavell cornered the title I really wanted for these few pages. He gathered his favourite pieces and called them Other Men's Flowers. All of us breathe the fragrance of lovely things that we have learned and have come to find priceless for us. Here are a few of mine.

Two Roads

I find that by nature I tend not to get too involved in might-have-beens. You know yourself how you get to thinking about your life. You find yourself remembering some particular point at which things could have gone so differently. If only a certain person had responded differently. If only a certain job had opened up at that particular time. If only you had known that such and such was going to happen when it did.

The interesting thing of course is that, when we do that sort of remembering, we are always apt to think of possibilities lost, which are then thought of as better possibilities than the reality we finally experience. But of course, there are also many points along the way when the choice that did become reality saved us from something perhaps worse.

This thought came to mind because of reading again one of the most famous of Robert Frost's poems.

> Two roads diverged in a yellow wood,
> And sorry I could not travel both
> And be one traveler, long I stood
> And looked down one as far as I could
> To where it bent in the undergrowth;
>
> Then took the other, as just as fair,
> And having perhaps a better claim
> Because it was grassy and wanted wear . . .
>
> I shall be telling this with a sigh
> Somewhere ages and ages hence:
> Two roads diverged in a wood, and I —
> I took the one less traveled by,
> And that has made all the difference.

from The Poetry of Robert Frost

Children

I met someone the other day who lived next door to us a fair number of years ago. We were at that time both in the navy and both living in Halifax, Nova Scotia. I always remember them for a silly reason. We were not long married, and we had no children. They had one, a four year old girl. I remember one day looking at them as parents, trying to imagine what it would be like to have a four year old child and to be responsible for that new life. At that time it seemed a great and mysterious responsibility.

Well, there are now young adults all over our house, and being responsible for a single four year old is no longer either mysterious or awe-inspiring. But the other day I thought again of those very famous lines of Kahil Gibran. They put perfectly something we all have felt.

Your children are not your children.
They are the sons and daughters of Life's longing for itself.
They come through you but not from you,
And though they are with you yet they belong not to you.

You may give them your love but not your thoughts,
For they have their own thoughts.
You may house their bodies but not their souls,
For their souls dwell in the house of tomorrow, which you cannot visit, not even in your dreams.
You may strive to be like them, but seek not to make them like you.
For life goes not backward nor tarries with yesterday.

You are the bows from which your children as living arrows are sent forth.
The archer sees the mark upon the path of the infinite, and He bends you with His might that His arrows may go swift and far.
Let your bending in the archer's hand be for gladness;
For even as He loves the arrow that flies, so He loves also the bow that is stable.

from *The Prophet*,
by Kahlil Gibran.

Real

In recent years the word *real* began to get a lot of use. We say, "He or she is not for real" or "I am desperately searching for the real me." We most frequently use it in connection with human character or personality or identity.

Strangely enough, or perhaps not strange at all, it is in a child's book that I came across the loveliest reflection I have ever heard. It is a definition of the word *real*, and it occurs in *The Velveteen Rabbit* by Margery Williams. The rabbit and the toy wooden horse are chatting one night as they stand together in the child's nursery.

"What is REAL?" asked the Rabbit one day, when they were lying side by side near the nursery fender, before Nana came to tidy the room. "Does it mean having things that buzz inside you and a stick-out handle?"

"Real isn't how you are made," said the Skin Horse. "It's a thing that happens to you. When a child loves you for a long, long time, not just to play with, but REALLY loves you, then you become Real.". . .

"Does it happen all at once, like being wound up," he asked, "or bit by bit?"

"It doesn't happen all at once," said the Skin Horse. "You become. It takes a long time. That's why it doesn't often happen to people who break easily, or have sharp edges, or who have to be carefully kept. Generally, by the time you are Real, most of your hair has been loved off, and your eyes drop out, and you get loose in the joints and very shabby. But these things don't matter at all, because once you are Real you can't be ugly, except to people who don't understand."

"I suppose *you* are Real?" said the Rabbit. And then he wished he had not said it, for he thought the Skin Horse might be sensitive. But the Skin Horse only smiled.

"The Boy's Uncle made me real," he said. "That was a great many years ago; but once you are Real you can't become unreal again. It lasts for always."

Master and Servant

I was visiting in the house, and I noticed the elderly dog. She was held in great affection because she had grown up with the family. Now she was walking with difficulty, and her other faculties were all leaving her. I couldn't help but refer to a poem of Rudyard Kipling, which I think is one of the most touching pieces of writing about the relationship of dogs and humans. It seems to me it deserves to be more widely known. Here are a few verses of it.

Master, this is Thy Servant. He is rising eight weeks old.
He is mainly Head and Tummy. His legs are uncontrolled.
But Thou hast forgiven his ugliness, and settled him on
    Thy knee . . .
Art Thou content with Thy Servant? He is very comfy
    with Thee.

Master — again Thy Sinner! This that was once Thy
    Shoe,
He has found and taken and carried aside, as fitting
    matter to chew.
Now there is neither blacking nor tongue, and the
    House-maid has us in tow,
Master, remember Thy Servant is young, and tell her to
    let him go!

Master, pity Thy Servant! he is deaf and three parts blind.
He cannot catch Thy Commandments. He cannot read
    Thy Mind.
Oh, leave him not to his loneliness; nor make him that
    kitten's scorn.
He hath had none other God than Thee since the year
    that he was born.

Lord, look down on Thy Servant! Bad things have come
    to pass.
There is no heat in the midday sun, nor health in the
    wayside grass.
His bones are full of an old disease — his torments run
    and increase.
Lord, make haste with Thy Lightnings and grant him a
    quick release!

Clouds

I look out of the window across the heaving wilderness of the clouds. We are at a height not quite above them all. Sometimes they are around us and then we emerge from them again, bursting into the sun.

Clouds are another country. They can create all the attributes of a strange and fantastic land. In an hour they can build a castle and set it high on a white mountain. They can erect whole ranges of hills. They can welcome your tiny flying chariot into great valleys. Clouds can play a vast game with sunlight, flashing it from their crests, deflecting it from one white precipice to another. Clouds are another planet, so near to earth yet stranger and more magnificent than anything our fiction can dream of. They have power, power to toss and tumble our craft with all its steel and computers and invention. Suddenly they release us and say farewell, and we turn down for familiarity and the distant greenery.

I find myself thinking of some lines of Shelley.

I am the daughter of earth and water,
And the nursling of the sky;
I pass through the pores of the ocean and shores;
I change, but I cannot die.
For after the rain when with never a stain
The pavilion of heaven is bare,
And the winds and sunbeams with their convex gleams
Build up the blue dome of air,
I silently laugh at my own cenotaph,
And out of the caverns of rain
Like a child from the womb, like a ghost from the tomb,
I arise and unbuilt it again.

Cargoes

The great four-masted schooners sailed into the harbour with a certain majesty, and as they came in to be received and surrounded by the mountains, they passed other ships. They passed the great grey steel ships that wait, turning on every tide with a passive resignation, for the grain shipments from the prairies. These waiting ships have edges. They are angular, sharp, utilitarian. They have skeletal derricks like brittle bones showing. They do not seek wind nor need it. They savage the ocean, driving at it to fulfil a schedule.

As I looked at these two creatures of the ocean, I couldn't help recalling how the contrast was put so perfectly by John Masefield, that great poet of the sea. Perhaps you know it. It's called "Cargoes," and to this day I remember the afternoon when a great English master helped me to discover it in school.

Quinquireme of Nineveh from distant Ophir,
Rowing home to haven in sunny Palestine,
With a cargo of ivory,
And apes and peacocks,
Sandalwood, cedarwood, and sweet white wine.

Stately Spanish galleon coming from the Isthmus,
Dipping through the Tropics by the palm-green shores,
With a cargo of diamonds,
Emeralds, amythysts,
Topazes, and cinnamon, and gold moidores.

Dirty British coaster with a salt-caked smoke stack.
Butting through the Channel in the mad March days,
With a cargo of Tyne coal,
Road-rails, pig-lead,
Firewood, iron-ware, and cheap tin trays.

Needs

I first named these few pages "Vulnerabilities," but it seemed somehow too contrived a word. Yet that is what these pages are about, those areas of life where none of us feels strong, where no matter what armour or mask we wear in daily life, we can be pierced by the "slings and arrows of outrageous fortune."

Giants

We still have somebody in our house who is interested in a story before going to sleep. Indeed, so are we all. No matter what age we are, as we reach for the book on the bedside table, we are reaching for a story, for another world that has never ceased to intrigue us. Still, I feel that we can never quite realize the power and significance of the story that we tell a child. I remember discovering this when I found a little book that is, for all I know, now out of print. It was called *Johnny and the Six Dreadful Giants*. It told of Johnny who was sent a letter by the king. The king wrote to Johnny that he wanted him to come to the palace. With the letter the king had sent a parcel, and in the parcel was a sword and a map. The king had written a note to Johnny saying that he would need the sword to fight the giants he would meet on the way to the king's castle.

I think if we went through that little book once, we read it a dozen times. Why? Because it is the story of life itself, its journey, its search for *home* in all the meanings of that word, the giants we wrestle with, and the defences and resources we have to develop. A child is fascinated because something down deep in the psyche knows that this is his or her own journey, that there are and will be giants to encounter. Perhaps above all, what is the real gift of the story to the child is that it enables him or her, through the story, to realize that the giants *can* be conquered. To the degree it does this, the story becomes far more than a pleasant way of sending the child to sleep. Rather the story opens a door by which insight, even without the child knowing it, enters his or her life. The story becomes therapeutic. It becomes a grace, a source of strength for living.

The Third Child

I have just mentioned the power and significance of a story for a child. The stories that have real power to keep attention are those that have been told again and again; this is fascinating. A few months ago I picked up an attractive copy of the complete stories of the Brothers Grimm. I thought somebody might be beyond them, but it turned out that he was not.

I notice how often in fairy tales, as we call them, there is the device of the "third child." You know how it goes. There is a dragon or an evil prince or a treasure. Three sons of the house go on the search or the attack. The first is brilliant, the second is strong. Both should succeed, but both fail. The third son is always in some way limited. Sometimes he is weaker, sometimes smaller or duller. You know from your experience of these stories, however, that it is he who will kill the dragon, conquer the villain, marry the princess.

After all that is told, why does a child roll over and begin to sleep contentedly? The answer is that, of course, the story isn't about a faraway third child in a long ago medieval world. The story is about the listening child. The child dwells in a land of dragons and villains and giants. Everything is larger, stronger, louder, richer than he. All around him are the older brothers and sisters, whether in his own family or in others. Suddenly his sense of smallness and weakness and lessness is given a message in the old story. The message says that maybe, in spite of all that feeling of being low on the totem pole, he can do things, he can achieve, he can slay dragons. Who knows, the sense of self-worth and confidence that we so often desperately seek in adult life may well be sparked by the memory of the third son or daughter, the weak one, the vulnerable one, but the one who gained the prize, slew the dragon, found the treasure.

Illness and Friendship

The conversation was about something that every one of us at some stage faces. You have certain friends, it may be another couple or a single person, it doesn't matter. You hear through the grapevine that there has been bad news about health. Something is threatening. You hear it through the grapevine because of a peculiarly new fact of modern relationships. We all know many people of whom we use the loose modern phrase "friends," yet we don't know them intimately, we don't meet them very often, and we may have only a few aspects of our two worlds in common.

So you hear that someone is seriously ill. You may choose to back off entirely. All sorts of wonderful reasons for doing this comes to mind. But if you decide otherwise (as did the person with whom I was chatting) how does one handle it?

When asked how to handle it, I in turn asked two questions. Does the person who is ill realize how serious it is? The answer was Yes. Does the person realize that you as friend know how seriously ill they are? Again the answer in this case was Yes. Then I made a suggestion. Pick up the telephone and say something quite simple and straightforward such as "I hear you've been through the mill. Can I drop over sometime and say hello." This does a couple of things. It gives them a choice about your offer. It lets them know that you care enough to hang in where a lot of people let go. It tells them that, if you do get together, they won't have to expend energy and nerves on pretending and wearing a mask. Incidentally neither will you. It's not a bad method.

Transition

We were chatting about a decision. It's a very difficult one, and since it is highly possible that most of us are going to have to make it, maybe we should share it.

You are, shall we say in our modern euphemistic way, no longer as young as you used to be. For a number of years you have lived alone in reasonable comfort. Your house is pleasantly located, and you have enjoyed the years of caring for it. You have a pet or two perhaps, a hobby, a number of good friends moving through the same stage of life as you, and some family whose younger lives you enjoy as interludes in your own quiet existence.

But now you have been ill for a while. You have been ill before, and friends and family have helped you through. But this time it has been longer, and that familiar recuperation has not quite worked this time. Somehow everything feels more demanding. Getting around, staying awake, concentrating on things, remembering things.

For the first time there is the dawning realization that maybe the time for a decision has arrived. You realize that others have been hinting at it. Maybe you just cannot live alone any longer. It's a great and significant climactic moment that our modern world has added to the sequence of life. It's a moment we must all be sensitive to in others and in ourselves. It's a moment of dying inside. But when the decision eventually is made, and when the transition to community living is accomplished successfully, it is also wonderful sometimes to see a new lease on life begin in somebody's face and eyes and voice, in fact, in their whole being.

Bereavement

Let me describe in quick vignettes some human situations.

They have lived in a middle-sized Ontario town for fifteen years. He is suddenly transferred to the coast. There are moving vans and parties and house-finding — the lot. But for a year things go wrong. He and she find their marriage tested, the children change, tears come easily, sleep patterns change, feelings about people are mixed.

They are twenty-five years married. Both children are at university. One day he announces that he has found somebody else and he wishes to go. After the dreary legal positions have one by one been gone through, there is a house for sale. She is being retrained for a profession she left years ago, and she finds life is an emotional rollercoaster.

He feels entrenched in the firm. He has been there for fifteen years. He knows the ropes. Things are tough at the moment, but everybody is hanging in there, and anyway it's tough all over. One day the phone rings, there is a lunch appointment or an office chat. Maybe there is not even a phone call, only a crisp letter, and he realizes it is all over. Even if there is another place to go to, funny things happen — sleeplessness, depression, tension.

What is the common factor in all these human situations? I suggest it is the process we call bereavement. But, you say, nobody has died. No, but a certain dying has happened in each case. A dying inside, of ego, of self-image, of self-confidence, of self-esteem, of friendships, of security, of familiar things. Recently I heard a woman, a doctor who has been a member of a healing team in a large hospital in London, England. She said that bereavement is "moving from a known way of life to an unknown way of life."

Maybe we should be aware that all around us there are many people experiencing bereavement, even though there are no funerals and no visible deaths.

Bad Company

I came across something the other day that made me think a lot. It is a famous incident in the life of Carl Jung. A professional man came to Jung suffering from a nervous breakdown. His story was simple. He had been working fourteen hours a day, and his nerves were shot. Jung's suggestion to him was very simple. He told the man to begin a regime where he worked only eight hours a day, and then went home and spent the evening alone and quietly.

The man was desperate; so he followed Jung's advice to the letter. He did his eight hours, went home, had his supper, went into his study or den. He stayed there for a number of hours. While he did, he played some of Chopin's music and read part of a Herman Hesse novel. The next day he carefully did the same. This time he read some Thomas Mann and played some of Mozart's music. On the third day he went back to Jung.

When Jung asked him how he felt, he said he felt just as awful as he had before. The doctor asked him what he had done. The man told him. "But," said Jung, "I said that you were to be alone with yourself. Not with Herman Hesse and Chopin and Thomas Mann, and not even with Mozart. I wanted you to be all alone with yourself." The effect of Jung's outburst crushed the man. "But Dr Jung," he said, "how can I be alone with myself. I cannot think of any worse company."

Jung looked at him and said something that has become a classic remark. He said quietly, "Yet this is the self you inflict on other people fourteen hours a day?"

As I said, that made me very thoughtful, and I thought it worth sharing.

Marriage

It is fashionable nowadays to say that the institution of marriage is very fragile. I heard somebody saying this again the other day as they discussed the separation of two people very much in the public eye. Hardly a day goes by but one doesn't hear of two people one knows withdrawing from marriage. Sometimes it will be within a few years of the marriage's beginning, or sometimes it will be at the second most likely stage, when the children are grown and almost on the point of leaving or have already left.

The truth is that neither is marriage any more strong or fragile than it ever was, nor are we as a generation more careless or contemptuous of it. There are I think other factors.

Human life has always been lived on three levels. There is the personal level, that of relationships. Of these the most complex and intimate is marriage. There are also the public or social levels, our working lives. In an age like ours the public and social levels of life are extremely oppressive. We live daily with psychological monsters. Much threatens the world. Many problems seem insoluble. Existence is extremely competitive and shows no signs of becoming less so. Therefore, in this decade there is a tremendously intense compensatory investment being made in the other two levels of our lives, our own personal interior journey and the relationships which help that journey. We demand so much of both of these levels of life that sometimes they buckle under the strain. Sometime we buckle inside, sometimes marriages or close friendships buckle. This is by no means the only reason, but it is, I think, a valid one. Marriage is under pressure not because we look to it for less but rather because we demand of it far more.

Checking the Children

If you have brought up a family, you know that for years in your life the last thing you do at the end of the day is check the children. Cats have to be put out, dogs have to be walked, a door locked, whatever your pattern is or was, but the children were checked. Nowadays there is only one person in our family whom I check, and perhaps he wouldn't appreciate it if he knew. Maybe I should just stop doing it, but you know how it is.

I sometimes think that one reason to keep on doing it is the quality of that particular moment when you see your child asleep. I find that it need not be merely in their years of infancy but as long as they are around. What does one see? What is it that fascinates? There is the serenity of youthful sleep, the abandoned posture. There is the vulnerability of life, of a particular life that is part of your life. This too is what you see in that moment. Perhaps also there is the contrast of seeing what is intensely alive and active and vibrant now absolutely still.

I suppose that, above all, there is the fascination of looking at your sleeping child and knowing that you are observing part of your very self. This is similar to those strange moments people have when they seem to be outside their bodies looking down at themselves. There in your child's features are nuances and glimpses of yourself. Of course, mixed in with those nuances are the strengths and the weaknesses that you know so well; and you know also that this sleeping life will have to do its own battling with them, and will have to experience its own joys and sorrows. You realize that in some sense you now can be only a spectator.

I am sure that all these things have gone through your mind. As they do so, you put the light out and you leave the room.

Laughter

Well, what do I say? This title needs the least elaboration of any. But for some reason, in the early days of this Journal, *I was very wary of bringing humour into its pages. Perhaps I was being too much the sombre philosopher. As time went on, it somehow became easier. I realized that, even if someone were listening in sickness or despair, perhaps a smile in life was what they most needed. Hence these whimsical thoughts.*

X-Ray

I recently had to go for an X-ray. It occurred to me that we often speak of "having faith" in your doctor. That's an excellent thing. I fully agree. But there is a fundamental difference between X-ray doctors and (begging their pardon) normal doctors. It is simply this. In the case of your normal doctor, you can at least see him or her. There he or she is, huddled in front of you at the tiny desk, a little baggy-eyed if it's late afternoon. Well, that's reassuring too. But in the case of X-ray doctors, you have to have quite a different degree of faith. It is not unlike the problems of believing in God, because a property that both God and radiologists have in common is that they are invisible.

I presume that, if you stayed all day, you might see a radiologist now and then. I like to think that they have corporeal existence, that they can be seen dashing from car park to elevator as dawn breaks. I like to think that in mid-morning they too reach with eager and even sometimes trembling hand for a steaming cup of coffee. Yet alas, I cannot vouch for any of this. I cannot say that I have any empirical evidence. All I can determine is that the technician keeps on putting exposed plates into a hole in the wall, and when she opens it to put in more, it is empty. Naturally then, I believe that a benevolent hand empties it.

Even the Old Testament heroes have an easier time than I in their pursuit of proof. It is said that Moses was allowed to see what the Bible calls "the back side of God," and that Moses' face shone for three days. I have never yet seen hide nor hair of a single radiologist in the office. I cannot guarantee my face would shine, but at least it would put my lingering doubts to rest.

The Gown

I have to report a minor triumph for the dignity of what, in more chauvinist days, would be called man. And since the consequences of this minor triumph will benefit the human race as a whole, it can indeed be regarded as for the dignity of all persons.

My tale concerns the garment that each of us has to wear at certain times in our lives when we fall into the hands of the medical fraternity. Before they do anything to you, they ask you to don something named with ultimate irony a hospital "gown." Nothing less like a gown can be imagined. In my time I have wrestled with this awful object. Alone recently in the cubicle of a radiologist's office, standing with this thing thrust into my hand, I found myself thinking of the vast achievements of humanity. We have conquered Everest, reached the moon, transplanted hearts. Surely, I thought, it is possible to bring to bear on the modern hospital gown that same greatness of the human mind and spirit.

I began analytically. The heart of the problem is that the gown, when put on, is in theory fastenable down your back. The fact, of course, is that this is humanly impossible. Very frequently the last inhabitant of the gown has already, in their fear and frustration, ripped off the lowest and therefore most strategic tie, and it has not been replaced.

Suddenly, in the fashion of many great scientific breakthroughs, inspiration came. I resolved what I should do. I would tie the ties before I put the thing on. I proceeded to do so. With care and a growing sense of achievement I got it on over my head. It was a moment of great triumph. So Alexander Graham Bell must have felt at the first phone call, Marconi facing the Atlantic in Newfoundland, "stout Cortez gazing with eagle eye at the Pacific." With bursting heart I left the cubicle. I was filled with the spirit of the true pioneer. However, just in case, I kept one hand behind my back. After all, even pioneers have to hedge their bets!

The Saucer

The longer I move around this particular three-score years and whatever which I am allotted, the more I appreciate the odd little episode that can, if you wish, be dismissed as crazy and childish. But I would bet a great deal that you have such moments too, if you wanted to admit them.

I like a cup of tea, especially a good cup of tea, preferably with a little milk and, although I feel more and more guilty about it, a little sugar. Well, the other day I made one. I was at home. There was nobody else around. And when I made the tea I somehow knew that it was a very good cup. Then I suddenly felt really thirsty. I wasn't interested in sipping this tea. I wanted to take it down in a great luxurious draught. But, you see, I couldn't because it was fresh and hot. On the other hand, to put more milk into it would destroy the very quality that was making it a first class cup of tea.

I was overcome by a terrible temptation. The moment it came on me, all sorts of childhood voices began to shout out, "No! you just don't do that!" I looked around. The dog was watching me. Through its sad eyes all the parents and teachers and aunts and uncles of my past looked in sorrow. I steeled myself. I took the cup, poured the magnificent tea into the saucer, and drank and drank and drank. Yea, did I drink even a second saucer, for by this time I was quite given over to being a sinner. Believe me, it was magnificent. Try it. Actually, it is the way they drank tea when Walter Raleigh first brought it home to England. All the best people did it. Who knows, if enough of us do it again, maybe all the best people will do it again. Terrible thought. I know I won't do it again for years, but it was very, very good.

Banks

I am beginning to suspect something. Even to think it under-
mines all my concepts of a safe and stable and trustworthy
world. I am beginning to wonder if, after all, my bank is
really on my side.

My bank is a friendly place. They smile at me, at least most
of the time. They say intimate things that make me feel unique and appreciated and known. Things like "How are you
today" and "Have a nice day" and "Have a nice weekend."
Things like this make one feel that one is more than a face in
the crowd, if you know what I mean.

My bank is always full of cheerful notices telling me how
much interest I will get if I do this or that with something it
calls "savings." Some day I am going to ask the manager what
this mysterious thing called "savings" is. My bank wants me
to buy a house. It has a picture of people doing just that. It is
also anxious for me to trade in my old car and buy a new one.
You can always tell the seasons in my bank. All the pictures
will change, and there will be new pictures telling me to buy a
speed boat or ski lessons or a holiday in Hawaii.

Another thing my bank keeps on trying to do is to help me
get organized with my money. It invents all sorts of new
ways for me to do this. It sells me a wallet of cheques so that I
cannot go wrong. When this doesn't work, it designs two
accounts for me, sometimes three. Since this hasn't worked
either, I see that for a small sum of money I can buy a special
new wallet with a duplicate cheque system. I buy it hoping
that this will finally organize me.

But I am beginning to think that the bank likes me just as I
am, never quite caught up, eternally dependent on its kindness, its helpfulness, and its generosity. Thank goodness
there are still things we can trust and depend on; don't you
agree?

Christmas Tree

We make the decision by the timing of some kind of instinctive tribal clock. This is the day. We gather as many of the family as possible. We are about to buy the Christmas tree.

It was not always thus. Once upon a time, when I was more innocent in the art of parenting and, of course, when I was more powerful because everybody was smaller and younger — in those days of innocence, I would buy the tree. Oh yes, small fry would come, but the wisdom and perception of Father was in those long ago days unquestioned. When he placed the tree on the car, there would be unquestioning and uncritical cries of excitement. When we came home, these cries of euphoria would continue as the tree was decorated. Here was where the maternal gifts (at least in those days) came into play. Man the hunter had dragged home the tree; woman the keeper of the cave (I will be torn limb from limb for this, in these more enlightened days) now made it a beautiful and shining thing. Even then there would be the odd remark from my other half to the effect that the tree was not, shall we say, perfectly formed.

However, in recent years I have changed the plan. As time passed, each of my chosen trees was received with less euphoria and more criticism. The tree was too high, too low, too wide, too narrow. There were yawning gaps in its branch system. Its trunk was warped. It was too cheap, too expensive, too large, too small. So I have changed. Chastened by criticism I now stay in the background. I drive the family to the lot. As they handle every tree in sight, I hang around vaguely. When they are all happy, they go through the motion of getting my opinion. I don't argue. I just ask how much the tree costs, and then I pay for it. After all, that is what fathers are for. Then I haul it to the car and strap it on. That too is what fathers are for. But even though I have had my moment of self-pity, I really enjoy it all very much.

Medieval World

Long ago in Europe there was a world very different from ours. If you walked the streets of it, you could tell that it was a society utterly stratified. You could tell that every person in the society had his or her own particular function which fitted into the whole. You could tell at a glance who was most important and who was least important. For the most part, the way you could tell all this was by the different types and colours of clothing. Here was a countryman or serf in sacking, here a merchant or clerk in sober grey, here a baron clip-clopping by us with his guards, here an elderly abbot or archbishop weighed down with vestments.

Well, I thought that that was all long ago, but I realize that such places exist to this day. They exist within our modern cities like neo-medieval towns. Their streets are long and straight and well-lit. People live in neat houses whose doors are almost always open. And up and down those quiet but busy streets go all the rigidly graded feudal levels of modern medical humanity, for as you may have guessed, I am speaking of a great city hospital.

There they all go, every thing and everybody you can tell and define by their dress. Every function is graded, coloured, labelled. There is the drink pourer, the bed maker, the back washer, the temperature taker. There is the maintenance staff, the nursing staff, the operating room staff. They mingle and weave in and out like members of ancient jealous guilds of long ago. Moving among them all are the barons, the nobles of this little medical city. Sometimes they move alone, sometimes like ancient nobles they are followed by attentive outriders, alert to the great man or woman's every whim. Yet unlike his medieval predecessor, who signified authority by his dress, this figure is the worst-clad in the whole hierarchical structure. He passes by, forehead bound in tight green, baggy white-ish coverings on the rest of him; out behind him swishes an ancient and sizeless coat of, dare I say, lincoln green. As he passes me, I accord him respect, for he or she may have given the gift of life to someone else within the hour. Yet there he goes, trailing, as you might say, clouds of un-glory!

My Tailor

When I read, as all of us do sometimes, that soon all the normal activities and transactions of life will be done by computer, I smile. The reason I smile is that no computer could possibly understand how human beings work.

Take me and my tailor. Now I don't really have a tailor in the luxurious sense. I am a size 42 tall in the January sales. But when I want pants or a pocket repaired, I go to a certain address.

Here's how it goes. I take in the pants and I explain the problem. Just before leaving I say, "Well, when do you want me to check in for it?" He says, "Oh, about the middle of the week." So the middle of the following week comes. I let it go for another couple of days, and then I lift the phone and I ask, "Did you get a chance to get at those pants?" He says, "No, but when do you want them for?" I say, "Well, I wear those a fair bit for work" He says, "Okay, I'll do them early in the week, say Tuesday."

Tuesday comes. We both know the next move. This time I drop in while passing. Dropping in while passing is less threatening than going in, if you understand what I mean. I ask how the pants are going. He says, "Right, I was just going to do it. Could you come back?" So we decide that I will come back at 5:30. But the game requires one more move. I don't go back at 5:30. I go back two days later. He is just finishing the pants. We chat about things, and we part the best of friends. The pants have taken three weeks, but nobody is insensitive enough either to say that or to apologize for it. We both knew it would take three weeks. But we are reasonable men; so we invent a fiction. We perform a series of exquisitely balanced acts of psychological ballet. Each knows the script. Not a word or a nuance is out of step. We relate to each other like two Japanese samurai who are both resolved that neither contestant will lose face.

Is it any wonder that I smile when I read that computers will one day manage all the transactions of our lives? I don't believe it for a moment.

A Magnetic Corner

North American television, in its annual thrashing around to get that magic thing called a new idea, has discovered something that a man named Ripley discovered many years ago. He called it "Believe it or not," and you know as well as I do that it became familiar in countless newspapers and magazines.

The television people have a program called *That's Incredible*. Recently I came in on the family watching it, and the program had everyone agog with the story of a hill in the eastern United States which is very strange because cars seem to free-wheel up it. It is called a magnetic hill. There is also one in Nova Scotia. They are among nature's freakish things.

But it made me realize something. In our house we have a most extraordinary area. It's a certain corner of the kitchen. In this corner there lie perpetual but ever changing collections of objects. There will be shoes, a frisbee, school books, a raincoat, a pile of magazines — the list goes on forever. Now the extraordinary thing is that nobody knows how these objects get into this corner. I have time and time again taken an object or, in moments of savagery, all the objects. I have arranged them in an accusing pile at mealtime, and tried to find out who placed any one object in that corner. Invariably each family member proves conclusively the impossibility of their being at fault. I retire defeated.

I can only conclude that we possess in our home one of nature's phenomena — a magnetic corner. Some night I am resolved that I will stay up all night. I will sit in the darkness and watch the various objects slide silently into that corner from various parts of the house. Check your own house. I suspect, and if you have a family I am quite certain, that there is a magnetic corner in your house. Check it out. It could get you on television!

Safe as a Church

In the endless analysis of the recent election, full of those wonderful insights that come so richly and so tantalizingly after the event, I was really intrigued by a tossed off remark made by that man of many tossed off remarks, John Crosby. Now Crosby was becoming the enlivener of Parliament's endless drone, the wit to whom we looked for the quick turn of phrase, a rotund if not always elegant Disraeli.

I was taken with a phrase he used as he post-mortemed the election. He said, "We (meaning the Conservative Party) thought we were as safe as a church." I presume he meant safe from serious challenge by the other parties. But, good heavens, look at that phrase, "safe as a church." Surely he couldn't mean that. Since when has it ever been safe to be a church? I have been in churches now for many a year, and I have yet to find a safe one. In fact there are almost always chronically unsafe things about a church. In small wooden ones on the prairies the stove is always about to explode in winter. In some the walls and windows are so porous and the doors so ill-fitting that the faithful are constantly smitten with pneumonia. In others the hassocks and cushions are so venerable and tattered that their contents spread all the allergies known to the medical profession. In some churches the preaching has been known to send people mad or make them so angry that they get heart attacks after their Sunday brunch. Even in huge cathedrals one is anything but safe. In really ancient ones gargoyles fall off, pillars crack. And of course there is always in every church, waiting for the unwary, that terrible threat of the collection plate. How in heaven's name could John Crosby have said that the government was "safe as a church." Well, the poor man found out exactly how safe that is!

Forbidden Territory

I wish to tell you about a mysterious and forbidden country. Once upon a time such places were beyond the Himalayas or at the sources of the Amazon. Not so today. I am sitting approximately ten feet from such an exotic land. It is called "First Class," and it is right here on this aircraft.

Like any forbidden country worth its salt, it is precisely that — forbidden. On pain of I am not quite sure what penalty, I am forbidden to enter. I am a citizen of another country called "Economy." Again, as in the tales of my youth, beautiful maidens draw the curtains which cut me off from that forbidden land. From time to time gleaming trolleys go by me, caravans of exotic edibles, only to disappear behind the curtains. Not for that mysterious hidden race is the plastic tray, the mass-produced steak. After a long interval the trolley returns through the veil of curtains. This time it is discreetly covered by white cloth, as if one of the inhabitants was being wheeled for surgery to some miniature first class operating room elsewhere in the plane.

Surely these people in such a land must be as gods. Surely they cannot line up for the washroom as we do. Yet when we land, I see a strange thing happen. When the curtains part and the lights go on and the cold wind from the airport slithers into the plane, they emerge among us. And lo, I see that their eyes are just as blood-shot as mine, their pants and jackets just as wrinkled as mine are. As we scramble through the exit, clutching briefcases and fat little bags that fit under the seat, I know that these gods are mortal. I go upon my way content.

Colonel Potter and Captain Clark

I am sitting in the waiting area. I could read, that is if I hadn't already read in the train for most of this afternoon and continued to read in the bus as it lurched out from the city on the slowly clogging freeway. If there is an ironic word in the English language, it is the word *freeway* to describe that particular mode of travel in our benighted urban world. However, I disagree. I am here now, and instead of reading I watch the world go by in its endless procession of shapes and sizes, skins, hairdos, expressions, attitudes. I watch it carrying books, newspapers, bags, pets, children.

Suddenly a voice on the speaker system makes an announcement. "Will Colonel Potter and Captain Clark please go to the main departures area immediately?" I don't know why, but I cannot dismiss these two unknown and unseen characters. My mind, for some reason which I cannot explain, immediately portrays Colonel Potter as small and stout and florid. Captain Clark is tall, moustached, grim-faced, rather like the young Basil Rathbone of many years ago. They are in, as we used to say, mufti. Clark has a trench coat. They are on serious business. I ask myself if it is to prevent something or somebody from changing the country's history. What has happened that they must go to the main exit, and "immediately?" Are they even at this moment running down escalators only to see a great black limousine pulling away into the October dusk? Have Potter and Clark served Canada, or perhaps even the western world, on mysterious missions that the world knows nothing of? What are their real names? Are they that most elusive of things, a genuine piece of Canadian romance? But I must stop. Colonel Potter and Captain Clark are probably in reality on their way to Ottawa with the results of a government survey or some such agenda.

It is so rarely a romantic world. But isn't it fun to wish it were?

Journeys Abroad

If I were to become very rich — at some time or other we have all let our imaginations go free on this thought — I know that I would do some travelling. I have for instance never seen Chartres, Canterbury, Glastonbury, Lindisfarne. For some mysterious reason, probably connected with childhood romantic reading, I would like very much to see Khashmir, Macchu Picchu, and Pompeii. Some day, please God, I may do so, but for now, let these travels suffice.

Going Home

It was late evening, at least it was late for these fall evenings when the light begins to slip away and the air gets that chill, making us say silly nostalgic things like "I'm afraid it's no longer summer." This is a very human remark; it's a device by which we manage to cling a moment longer to the fact that summer has been.

It was late evening of a lovely day on the Oregon coast. On a short holiday it was that pleasant hour between the end of driving and the looking forward to supper. It was a time when the beach and the rocks and the wind and the gulls and the sea called and said, "A walk." So we took a walk. First we went to the edge of the land overlooking the beach.

There I saw him. For a moment I thought it was a rock. This is not surprising, of course, because nature designed him to hide among them in danger. But then I realized what he was. He lay on his back, his skin smooth, weathered by salt and age, his girth narrowing to the slim still head and face. His eyes were closed, his flippers rested almost like hands asking to be clasped. He was lying among some rocks in an open area of sand. He had not been there very long.

I don't know when this seal had died or how. I don't know whether he had just grown old and weak or whether sickness had struck. But the ocean had brought him here and the tide had retreated. He looked great and strong and rather noble. There was about him a dignity and a peace.

All that night the wind rose and the ocean thundered and the Moon pulled the great Pacific tides across the sand and the rocks. At some moment under the starlit darkness the sea reached out for him and took him home. There was no sign of him when we walked the shoreline in the sunlit morning.

Mount St Helens

An emotion that most of us, myself included, feel seldom at first hand is that of awe. We speak of being awed by this or that, it may be a hurricane or some huge man-made operation like the St Lawrence Seaway or the James Bay project. Very often, however, it is the concept rather than the actuality that awes us.

We are thirty-seven thousand feet over the American-Canadian border country. It is a beautiful late summer evening. We know, because we have been told a couple of hours ago, that once again Mount St Helens has blown. But even more exciting is the fact that we are turning south for a look at the volcano.

Over eastern Oregon we turn out toward the distant Pacific. Far below us the long shadows of evening are hiding the valleys and gilding the western slopes with gold. Suddenly we are there, passing over slightly to the south. The great gaping mouth of the volcano is hidden by its own vast and ponderous outpouring. The smoke comes out in a tortuous and twisting mass, uncoiling itself from the earth and then climbing up like a gargantuan pillar, until it begins to fall away into a cloud stretching far to the northeast. Because the sun is now lowering to the horizon, it pours in from the Pacific and sends shafts of light into the darkness of the smoke. Great caves of changing light are created within the column — orange, gold, scarlet. I feel that I want to capture this majesty and hold it forever. Of course I cannot. But I shall never forget this encounter with the terrible splendour of creation.

Parthenon

I have found what everyone seeks on the Acropolis at Athens, a secluded spot to sit and think. I come from two lands; those who have built this place knew neither of them. It is possible they knew of the faraway Atlantic island where I was born, though they would have known of it only as an infinitely distant and almost mythical place. Its inhabitants they would certainly have designated as barbarians! My other homeland across the western ocean might as well have been on the other side of the galaxy, as far as they were concerned.

Yet what grew here in this tiny spot, what was searched for and lived out on this rocky hill, has spread beyond either ocean and has created societies the Greeks could never have dreamt of.

It is difficult to describe what it is that makes the word *Greek* so full of meaning for the whole history of western civilisation. In some ways it is recognised best only by placing this city of Athens against the backdrop of the world of its time, and seeing the contrast.

There is too the sad fact of the transience of the glory of this place. If a visitor from outer space came to this Acropolis seven centuries before Christ, they would have seen a tribe barely subsisting. Two hundred years later a visitor would have seen a high civilisation. Three hundred years later, although the building still stood, the real glory was already beginning to become a memory. That glory would be recalled again and again in the long story of the western world. It would haunt us and call us to what it had once been. Today as I sit here looking across at the Parthenon, I realise that this is perhaps one of the most strategic spots on earth to listen to the voices of time.

Delos

I am walking the winding path to this lovely and silent place. An hour away by plane, a night's sailing away across the impossibly blue sea, is the noise and heat and tension of Athens. But this is Delos, where the tiny lizards of the island slip among the fallen stones and hiss for a moment before disappearing again among the broken walls and sunken pillars of the past. This is Delos, southeast of the mainland, where poppies grow in blood red profusion among the grass and rocks. They are of course, like all things in this magic world, not merely poppies. Here, even before the houses were built, even before the shrines and temples, here in the dawn of Greek imagination, this island was the habitation of gods. Among them was the young man Adonis. Here one day among long gone woods, attacked by a lion, Adonis' golden flesh was gashed. Where his blood spilled, the flowers were painted scarlet and the poppies were born.

Here too on Delos was born Apollo, son of Zeus, the god of love and kindness and of all human striving toward the good. Round his shrine the city grew and prospered.

Adonis and the poppies. Apollo and Zeus. We of course are moderns as we walk on this island. Most of us would smile at the gods and their adventures. And yet we would do well to realise that to be pagan, to see the world peopled with gods that give a higher level of reality to life's mystery, was infinitely healthier than the empty world and sky in which millions of today's inhabitants see themselves imprisoned. For through the gods the Greeks encountered, as indeed we all encounter, him who is God beyond the gods.

Constantinople

My mind says "Istanbul" but something deeper in me wants to reject that and instead to say "Constantinople." I suppose that way down in what Jung would call my race memory, Constantinople is western and Graeco-Roman, and is culturally my mother, while Istanbul is the sound of another history, more distant from my interior country, eastern, exotic, somehow, if I am honest, threatening.

It is early morning. All night we have steamed north from the blue Aegean to these waters. They are different, greyer even in the new day. Here in this great wide bay the Aegean and the Black Seas mingle. We are still standing out in the middle of the channel; so I can see the panorama that has fascinated travellers for two thousand years.

Below me in the water, bobbing and shunting, weaving in and out of each other's wakes, is the teeming maritime traffic. Tiny boats full of vegetables, varied cargo of every kind, shuttle hither and yon, a solitary figure at the back with hand on the tiller. Out from the western side emerges a grubby once-white ferry, pouring smoke, already laden with passengers for the Asian side and presumably for the day's work. Across the water are the old and new cities on the western bank, divided by the inlet known to the Venetians and the Ottomans as "the Golden Horn." The old city rises from the water in terraces. Along the water's edges a solitary railway line and a highway betray this hurrying century. They lie half hidden, seeming quite properly to apologise for their existence. Just then the sun catches some point of a minaret, and for a moment there is a flash of gold in this oldest of cities, and a tower of Byzantium blazes.

St Sophia

St Sophia. It stands amid the hot and dusty streets of Istanbul. The houses are chipped and peeling, the ill-kept city park with its dry and tufted grass is covered with scattered papers from unnumbered ice cream cones and candy bars.

St Sophia. Its outer walls echo the thunder of traffic, the shrill impatience of drivers blowing their horns, the shouting of hawkers, the clatter of soft drink sellers.

St Sophia. Sudden quietness on entering a courtyard. Then doors so massive that one reaches for a half-forgotten word — *cyclopean*. Inside the doors there is the same compulsion as in a gothic cathedral. You must look up. It's an instinct. As you do, you are both awed and repelled. You are awed as you see the mosaics of Byzantine craftsmen. The gold set into the wall glistens in the shadows. But all around is the crumbling of that art and that beauty. The enemies are dampness, time, the corroded air, and these enemies are everywhere.

St Sophia. One moves out from the walls, out under the great soaring dome. Everywhere on these walls there is the power struggle from the past. Here are Christian mosaics, the pictures formed stone-by-stone before the icon and the stained-glass window. Above them on the walls, the huge circular shields bear verses from the Koran in a giant script. Here two empires, two histories, two related yet antagonistic views of reality meet and wrestle. And above them all, far far up, half hidden in the shadows under the roof, is the Virgin Mother and her child, somehow triumphing gently over the mildew of time and the wars of men.

The Dardanelles

A moment of stillness, a thought to be shared, not because it is unique to me and not because there is any great revelation in it, but because it allows me to share an experience.

Ten-thirty at night. I am standing overlooking the forward lower deck. Beyond in the darkness is the white bulkhead of the bow, beyond that the lights of another ship coming to meet us and pass us in this channel. There is no sound except the muffled hum of the diesels far below, the swish and slapping of the bow wave creaming away into darkness.

We are moving through the Dardanelles, Istanbul behind. Before us, hidden in the night and waiting for the dawn, the islands of the Aegean, sun drenched and brown. But now there is only the night and its sounds and, over to the starboard side, lights along the dark and hidden coast. Near me I hear footsteps as someone walks slowly on the deck behind me.

This is not just any coast in the darkness. Before I was born other men stood on other decks and probed the darkness of this same stretch of water. They slept fitfully and dreamt of fearful possibilities soon to become actualities. They came from coasts beyond the farthest seas. They heard the sounds of this channel and thought of faraway faces. In the dawn they went ashore, wave after wave of them, and the sun shone on their mangled bodies. If I could pierce the darkness I would see the monuments erected so long ago. More than a quarter of a million men died here. We are passing Gallipoli, and the night sky is alive with stars.

Children of Two Worlds

In Hong Kong, between the great wall of high rises that face the water and the water itself, there is a wide heavily trafficked boulevard that is crossed at a couple of places by pedestrian bridges. When you cross, at least where I did, you are quite near one of the many harbour sections that serve different purposes. This particular section of water is a kind of floating image of the modern world.

First, in near the harbour wall to my left and right, there are the sampans. They are clustered together, moving slightly as the people move hither and yon from boat to boat. They form a dark coloured huddled mass on the water. Now and again a sampan will detach itself and move out among the lines and off into the great bay. There is a constant busyness, a ceaseless lifting of sacks and boxes, washing is hung to dry, children play. Obviously it is a little world, a community.

Beyond the huddled sampans you look over the outer part of this stretch of water. In front of you, gleaming white and chrome, reflecting the sun, riding at anchor, are scores of ocean going private luxury craft.

I suppose the reason the scene registered with me was because of a fleeting image I noticed. A sampan had detached itself and was threading its way out into the harbour. Standing at the bow was a small child. I'd say she was about four or five. And as the sampan passed beside one of these gleaming pleasure craft, another child appeared on its deck. Again, a small girl not very much older. For a moment they stood, only about twenty feet apart, and looked at each other until the sampan passed around the yacht's bow and headed out. As I turned away I felt that I had seen a symbol of the worlds that intersect here and elsewhere, and that will not go on for ever . . .

Empty Stage

I suppose that I have been in a fair number of theatres in my time. For some reason there is a particular one that haunts me. I once sat there in solitary silence. There was no box office, no play, no actors, no audience except myself. At least they did not exist in reality, but they existed for a few moments in my groping imagination.

The path to it leads through the ruined area of the town of Byblos in Lebanon. You are walking up a slope to where some trees are slanted from the breezes that blow in from the Mediterranean. You top the slope and there it is. It is very small. Twenty centuries ago a routine decision in the huge bureaucracy of Rome must have sent a man here as local representative. Who knows, he may have lived near here in his villa, but there is no trace of it. Even in his day the surrounding half-buried ruins would have been ancient.

He may have longed for a theatre he had left behind in Rome. However, for a reason we will never know, he chose this flat spot beside the trees overlooking the beach to build a small private amphitheatre. It holds about fifty people. You take your seat on the steps, and in front of you is the tiny stage.

I came to it in the late evening. The air was still warm, the area silent. I sat down. Behind the stage was the fall off of ground to the water. Beyond was the oldest and most romantic of seas, the Mediterranean. Did he once sit here with his family looking at a play newly received? Did they sometimes gaze, as I am now gazing, out to where the sun has gone down, thinking of Rome and its faraway seven hills? For a few more minutes I tried to people the seats and stage. I said softly one of the very few Greek expressions I recall from university, and then came away. And all the way down the slope I looked back.

Arriving at Ben Gurion

There are a few places in the world that have a kind of dual geography. They are not only places on the map, but they also exist as countries in the mind. For millions of people Israel is such a place.

It is not yet in my sight. Below me and to the right is the island of Cyprus. Beyond that I can see the dark metallic sheen of the eastern Mediterranean. Every now and again I look for the coast line. Seeing it I am aware of looking at a land that for millions of people in western society possesses a haunting quality. Down there in the evening dusk, which now hides all but its outline from me, something happened that can never be insignificant. Whether I am Christian or Jew, this holds true. Down there are roots, for one of us racial and spiritual, for the other spiritual. My childhood mind reached out in imagination for this land as voices fed me stories long ago. Those stories focussed on a figure and a face and a voice.

For all these reasons I am peering out of this vibrating window, looking down not on mere land but looking deep into myself. Yet an outer reality intrudes. As we pass south along the coast, lights begin to cluster. Slowly they spread to make the sea of lights which means a city. There is the gentle dipping of the plane, the preparation, the impact and the noises and confusion of Ben Gurion Airport. There are soldiers. One realizes that there have always been soldiers here. They carry guns. Once they carried spears. By some terrible law of history or destiny, life here has always been costly. We have arrived in Israel.

Crusader Church

Time is a mystery. It is many-layered, immense, immutable, and it commands and possesses our lives. We sing songs about it, write poetry, wrestle with its mysteries in our stories. In the middle east time spills around me like a great ceaseless fountain. I think of that again and again as I move about Israel.

Here I stand in the courtyard of a crusader church in old Jerusalem. I emerge from this repository of eight centuries of time, and I walk hardly a hundred yards across the stone before the earth drops away beyond a low wall. I am looking down into a major excavation. It has already been going on for some years, and it will continue for years more. Years, it seems to say, are not giants of time. Centuries, perhaps, millenia certainly are, but not years.

Deep down in the earth are signs of other builders, long ago plans, forgotten splendour. The pillars stand on either side of the emerging floor. There, emerging again from the stones and the earth, is the exciting and tantalizing glint of an old mosaic. Immediately you know that long before the crusaders built those great grey walls behind you, here at another level of earth and time others built. We call them the Byzantines. They came to this city seven centuries before the crusaders. They came searching for the places that for them were the holy memories of their faith. There they built their tribute long ago.

I stand here in my moment of time and pay my silent tribute on a pilgrimage that both Byzantine and crusader would fully understand.

Jericho

Slowly and painfully they came out of the desert and into the mountains. The brown empty valleys were ovens under the blazing sun. Some of the younger ones remembered no world other than this moonscape of desolation.

Then one day they came over the mountain range in this desolate land of Moab and looked out across a great flat valley floor. Below them stretched a huge pale blue lake, absolutely still as if painted there by a giant. The air above it undulated as vapour rose in endless evaporation. Far beyond and across the lake, running from north to south, was a high escarpment composed of rocky and barren mountains. There was no softening in this world, no pity for human weakness. Then you looked north and there it was. It lay dark green against the endless brown, huddled in dense and rich profusion, the buildings among the trees. The travellers from the desert long ago wanted it. They lusted after its life and its growth and its cool thirst-quenching loveliness, as it stood in some of the cruellest desert in the world. So they came down from the mountains, and they took it in blood and screams and death. They flung themselves into the spring that ran through the ruins, and they laughed and danced in the water.

I stand here today, thirty-two centuries later, the shade of an olive tree above me, my bare feet dipped in this same spring that glistens and murmurs under the blazing sun. It has come from the depths of the earth, and it has heard the crying and the laughter of countless generations. It makes me aware of my moment of life here on this ancient stage called Jericho.

Qumran

For the last few hours we have been standing in the excavated ruins of Qumran. They lie in the dust and heat and desolation of the Dead Sea area south of Jerusalem.

In these rooms and corridors a community worked and studied, before and after the life of Jesus of Nazareth. They believed that their world was disintegrating, and so they set out to design a microworld (as all communes set out to do) where life could be lived on their terms.

Among the things these people did — and by the way they were called Essenes — was their ability to copy beautifully and meticulously the scrolls that were the holiest objects in their culture. They did this until one day the Roman legions came and everything ended in Qumran.

But before it did, a group who had been prepared for this day took the jars containing the scrolls from the shelves and hid them. Those men left that cave and went back along the pass to Qumran and to death.

Days became weeks, weeks became months, months became years, years rolled into centuries. Minor earth tremours shook the area, sometimes rocking the now ancient jars and breaking them against one another or toppling them to the ground. But the cave mouth remained open.

One day in 1957 there was a shadow against the light of the cave mouth, and a goat scrambled in and lay down. Night came and went. In the morning a Bedouin goatherd stood on the other side of the Wadi, saw the cave, and pitched a stone into its dark mouth in search of his goat. In the silence of the morning, he heard the sound of something breaking. He scrambled down the almost sheer cliff face. There before him, preserved where jars had survived, was the lasting gift the men of Qumran had left to a future they could not even imagine. We call that gift the Dead Sea scrolls.

Megiddo

Even today its position is commanding and strategic. I am standing at the bottom of the slope leading to one of the world's great *tells* or mound of archaeological excavation. Here men and women have lived in cities from approximately 4000 BC. The earliest men and women we today label Neolithic. Yet underneath that neat dehumanizing label one knows that they watched this cloudless blue sky as I do, that their children shrieked in the ecstacy of cool water and chased a lizard among these rocks.

I am walking over Megiddo, this fortified city. It is calculated that there are twenty successive Megiddos buried under layer after layer of dust, humanity, time. Once this place was a border outpost of the Egyptian empire. From Megiddo we have the most elaborate correspondence discovered anywhere in the east. Fourteen centuries before Christ there was a man here who bore the responsibility of local government. He looked out through the gap in the ridge that I now face, and he saw an army advancing, a strange wandering people from the north which he called the Habiru and which centuries in his future would be called Hebrews. Desperately he sent messages for help. Today we have those quick military messages. They are still decipherable on the clay tablets he gave to a horseman who galloped south along the coast road.

Five hundred years went by, and another king invested vast amounts here. I am walking through the stables which could hold six hundred horses. That king's name was Solomon. Again, three thousand years later, another military governor chose this place for strategy and war. The date was 1917. The man was an Englishman named Allenby who afterwards took as his title Viscount Allenby of Megiddo. But his war and his life was only a flickering moment in the endless life of this hill called Megiddo.

The Border

I stand in the middle of this country road. On either side are the fields. A slight breeze rustles the grass. Beyond me a few hundred yards to the right is a deserted building. Straight ahead and about half a mile away, perhaps less, are smaller lower buildings that fringe the road as it narrows into the distance. They are only a few minutes' walk away on this balmy May evening in the Golan Heights in Israel. A few minutes' walk — yet they are as far away as if they were in another world.

Ten feet in front of me is the end of Israel. Beyond the barricade, seventy yards away, looking neither imposing nor effective, stands the hut here the United Nations patrol waits between the two — shabby, vulnerable, courageous. Beyond that is erected another barricade where Syria begins.

What strikes one is the terrifying ordinariness of this line of absolute division. There is complete absence of design. A wooden hut where two young men keep watch. They are warm and easy and smiling. They hold the black repeater rifle with easy familiarity. It is the briefcase of their particular business. At each end of the barrier there is an old oil drum weighted presumably with concrete, and between them is a bar. That's all. Far down the road there is a movement at the other border. I move to the gully at the side of the road to take a photograph of the area. I see a length of rusty barbed wire and beyond it a cluster of the scarlet poppies that grow wild in this area. Barbed wire and poppies, the universal symbols of war and tragedy.

Nazareth

Today, if you approach from the south, you come to Nazareth through the lovely rich fertile Vale of Esdraelon, then up the winding highway that climbs into southern Galilee. You take your choice of Nazareths, the new and the old. Yet even if you choose the old you will walk in a mingled time and culture. In narrow streets you will be brushed by a donkey laden with full sacks, and at the same time you will hear the latest popular music blaring from a transistor radio.

Mary walked in streets not very different from these. They are narrow and hot, rich with the many odours of food, of animals, of cooking, of garbage. Here in these streets she carried her child. Here he would have been born but for a bureaucratic decision taken a thousand miles away in Rome. Augustus the emperor decided to take a census for taxation purposes. A galley slipped out of Brundisium to Cyprus and Salamis. An army detachment took the diplomatic mail to eastern army headquarters in Antioch. From there a horseman took the sealed orders down the coast road to the procurator's residence and the government offices in Caesarea. From there the instructions filtered out into the villages and towns of the three provinces of Palestine — Judea, Samaria, Galilee. And so it came to the ears of Joseph the carpenter. Every man had to return to the place of his family origins. For Joseph that meant a journey south. Eighty-five long miles over tough and sometimes lonely terrain, no guarantee of safety or accommodation at the end. So Mary left these streets of Nazareth, and the stars watched as they headed south for the distant hills of Judea.

Night Over Asia

You lift off from Tokyo airport, and you swing in a wide arc over the sprawling giant below you. Down there is one of the largest centres of gathered human beings on this planet. Slowly you swing around until the great plane is heading south and west. For a while below you are the tiny endless lights of southern Japan. Somewhere down there is Hiroshima, the city which the human race, in one obscene and awe-inspiring explosion, used as a laboratory to experiment upon itself.

After a while you are out over the ocean. As you sail south in the gathering dusk, you know that to the west is the one remaining great community on earth which fascinates and mystifies because of the still unknown quality about it. Over there, stretching from this ocean to the Himalayas, is China, busily engaged in being born, yet as old as Rome and even older. Down there in that vast experiment one quarter of the human race is seeking answers to questions about the relationship of the individual and society. Some of those questions have been asked at terrible cost.

You move imperceptibly down along the coast of China, miles above it, detached, yet knowing that its future affects your life and the life of mankind. What is forming in one in four of the human race cannot but affect us all.

The seat trays click down for supper. It does not betray by its contents where you are on the earth. It is the food of that ubiquitous earth-encompassing realm, an empire in itself, the airlines. As you eat, the plane slowly moves around the great belly of the China coast. It slips lower in the sky, and the lights of ships appear in the China Sea. Suddenly there is a blaze of light, a twinkling of what seem vast chandeliers against the surrounding darkness. You drop still lower until the lights surround you and are flashing by. Suddenly you are in Hong Kong.

Travel

I hear that Willy de Roos is now far down south in the Pacific. You remember how he sailed his solitary journey through the North West Passage, slipped through the Bering Straits (if anyone ever slips casually through that far and lonely water), and came to visit Vancouver. Now we know of him because of his contact across the miles with a local ham radio operator.

I thought of Willy de Roos again as I picked up another book, the story of another sail hoisted to the ocean, a book called *The Brendan Voyage*. From that my mind went to Kon Tiki and to Frances Chichester and to all the endless terrifying challenges that have pitted men and women against the ocean.

Why mention such journeys? Because human beings are so built that journeying is never merely a whim or a madness. There is a spiritual quality about it. In the centuries of the Norsemen, the ocean was seen not only as a source of plunder but also the approach to Valhalla. In Celtic mythology the ocean was the world that led to the Isles of the Blessed. In the Middle Ages it was thought by many that somewhere there could be found the vast mouths of the four great rivers that ancient stories claimed led out of the Garden of Eden. They hoped that one day they might find the river mouth and rediscover again the long lost Eden from which Adam and Eve had been banished.

In a sense that longing is present in all of us, articulated or not. Whether it be a Willy de Roos being lifted up by a great Pacific swell, or ordinary folk like you and me looking toward our next trip, all of us have reasons for travel that are deeper and older and more mysterious than we realize.

Countries of the Mind

In this *Journal* I have often chatted about travelling. I suppose it has become very obvious that I travel with a kind of naiveté. I tend to travel (what little I have done) on two levels. One is the realm of actuality, where I can see quite clearly that the universal ability to travel is ironically happening at the same time as the standardising and homogonizing of the world. I can see very clearly that this process takes away from travel a great deal of reward. This of course can be overcome by avoiding our universal urban civilization, but very few of us have the money, the means, or the stamina to climb Kenchenjunga or to sail to Antarctica or up to the Amazon. But I digress. The other realm I tend to travel is the country of the mind, where I can entertain all sorts of associations, historical, literary, factual, fictional.

I think it is important to say that this is not avoiding contemporary reality and indulging in a kind of sentimentality and nostalgia for a so-called Golden Age or a fairy land. I find that I acknowledge the present and recognise it with all its mixture of agony and hope, promise and threat. But if the present of any place can also be seen in the context of centuries of its own past, then that place is seen and experienced not with less reality but even more. The next time you see Hawaii advertising itself in terms of free drinks and six inches more leg-room in "economy," read the opening chapters of James Mitchener and see the colossal majesty of a world rising from the young ocean in fire and thunder. That's something of what I mean.

The famous Dr Samuel Johnson was such a traveller. He once said that it was impossible to walk on the Island of Iona and not to be aware of the centuries of holiness that had been lived out there, or to stand on the field of the battle of Marathon and not to hear the thunder of chariot wheels. I think that too is something of what I mean.

The Kiss

You leave the city and head west. The countryside is rising in a series of gentle steps. The fields are varied. This is, for the most part, dairy farming country. After about seven or eight miles you see the sign to the left. This time the road is narrower but still meticulously paved. After all, people from every country in the world find their way here. Suddenly there are the outlying houses of the village, a small stone bridge, and you are there. The heart of it all is a little farther on, and so you go one more turn into the open area of the centre of the village, and now you are really there. Across the trees, beyond a small meandering stream, you can see the battlements.

There are of course the souvenir stall and the turnstile. It seems that they are the gateway to all history nowadays. You walk first by the little river, over a tiny bridge, across a field; then you are below the great wall. Climbing begins, at first gradually. You are not yet climbing inside the castle. You are only ascending the rise on which it stands. There is a narrow gate, the tiny stone opening, then the endless dark winding steps. Up and up, glancing out the slits in the wall, you climb. Up past the great banqueting hall and out onto the battlements. Over at the far end of the battlements there is the object of it all. There is much giggling and chatting. You approach the area. You decide. You lie down where millions have lain. You slide out and down through the gap, firmly held. You press your lips on the cold hard surface. They pull you back from the drop. Much laughter while all this is going on. Silly things said. Perhaps a photograph or two. You move away to look out over the green fields that roll away on every side from these battlements. You've done something silly yet universal and fun. You have just kissed the Blarney Stone!

Irons

I was, with countless others before and after me, moving as a sightseer through Warwick Castle. Our two youngest and myself were enjoying the dark delights of the dungeons. Warwick does the visiting small boy proud. It has more than one level of dungeon, and it includes a display of early torture instruments.

Its a cliché to say that there really is nothing new under the sun. What is not a cliché, but is something that should make us think long thoughts, is the fact that the most contemporary elements of that centuries-old tourist attraction lie in the dungeon area.

In one of the rooms there hangs an obscure contraption that was known simply as "irons." Underneath, printed neatly and expressed in a way calculated to give the tourist value for money, it explains how a man was placed in this body cage and hung in public until he died, often having first gone mad. Grown men, the notice says, who had withstood much more were known to break down even when only threatened with irons.

Grim history, the tourist says, and thinks of tea and sandwiches. Far from it. I quote the London Times from 25 July of this year. It describes the experience of a 27 year old Brazilian business man. Arrested by security forces for political activity two years ago, he has not yet had trial. We are speaking about a great and powerful modern country. I quote *The Times*: "Mr Verzola's interrogation is known to have included the use of electric shocks and the *pau-d-arara* (the parrot's perch, as it is called, in which the victim is suspended by an iron bar passed between the knees and the elbows)." So I walk out of the dungeon of ancient Warwick Castle, but it occurs to me that I cannot as easily walk out of twentieth-century life.

The Play

The Passion Play at Oberammergau has been going now once a decade for three hundred and fifty years. In thanksgiving for escaping the Plague the village made a vow to perform, every ten years, an enactment of the drama of the last days of Jesus of Nazareth's earthly life.

When you approach this Passion Play you have some difficulty in assessing it. It is not as simple as criticising a normal production of a play at, let us say, the Stratford Festival, yet in so far as Oberammergau's play is now an internationally known event, it cannot escape bearing increased critical reflection. One thing that strikes you as you watch the play is that characterization is largely absent. The figures have the simplicity of the cartoon or the parable. By using the word *cartoon* I am in no sense sneering at it. In cartoons and parables characterization is at a minimum. Instead there are *archetypes*. You have a bad man, a good man, a bad woman, a good woman, enemies or friends, love or hate, black or white, rich or poor.

In that kind of treatment there are moments in the play when the portrayal or motivation is over-simplified. This is particularly true in the treatment of such people as Caiaphas the High Priest.

You see, the real terror of the tragedy that Oberammergau acts out is not that evil men destroy a good man. The real terror is that we all live in a political world where all human actions are ambiguous, where most human decisions are made from what are thought to be the best motivations and for the best intentions.

Given its method, Oberammergau cannot portray that kind of subtlety.

The Puppets

To move through the endless rooms of the great architectural achievement called Isola Bella is to experience a long ago power trip. The vast palace completely covers the island in Lake Maggiore and is the creation of one of the great northern Italian families of the seventeenth century — the Borremeos.

As the morning moves on and you descend from the vast upper halls and galleries, you enter a succession of apartments built to be what the English language of that day might have called "conceits." Floors and walls and ceilings are covered with coral to give the feeling of their being vast grottos.

I am standing in one of these grottos where the walls are lined with glass cupboards. In these cupboards are hundreds of puppets. They are dressed in the clothes of the sixteenth and seventeenth century and represent the total gamut of daily life. Here is a whole travelling scene, the lord and his lady are in their coach surrounded by servants. Here is a dashing troop of soldiers of some great Italian family.

Here is the interesting cupboard. Suddenly the puppets change. Here under its glass is terror. The faces are gargoyles, the gestures grotesque, the limbs twisted. Skeletons, monsters, leering nightmare faces look out from the glass. Here, amid all this power and all this celebration of life above and around me, is the acknowledgement of death and fear and darkness. Here is the acknowledgement of vulnerability. Through these puppets the people must have acted out the dark side of their existence. I cannot help thinking that it says a lot for them that they faced it. On the whole we tend to hide it. But then the Borremeos had not yet discovered all the devices by which we manage to do our hiding.

De Medici

I am moving through the long gallery of this great palace of Isola Bella. It occupies the whole of an island in the calm and lovely waters of Lake Maggiore. In the long gallery, as was the fashion of earlier centuries, hangs this priceless collection of tapestries and paintings. Out from the canvasses gaze the faces of the succeeding generations of the family who built this place and who stamped their image so grandiosely upon it. They do not, I must say, look particularly noble. The faces of the men are for the most part sharp, ferret-like, graceless. Although they gaze down at me, rumpled and tourist-like as I am, I do not feel any crushing inferiority, the feeling that great portraits can sometimes give. No superior and finely chiselled countenance brands me tiresomely middle class, intruding on a nobility made vulnerable by time.

But here is a face that remains in the mind's eye. It is a woman. Her sudden presence makes me realize that the house of Borremeo apparently preferred to paint its males. But she won out. Why? I look down at the name. She is a de Medici from the south. How wise of some Borremeo to bring a de Medici home to this island. He brought with her the thing that was beyond all price in that graceful and yet savage seventeenth century world. She stands there tall and lovely, at least as her painter so made her.

I am looking at a marriage of power. Today it would be a merger between two great industrial empires. Headlines would be made. Stocks and bonds would rise. The long ago wedding was precisely that. Even after all the years, if you look in her eyes in this portrait, you realize she too knew that.

Bells

At the heart of almost every city in Europe, certainly in all the old cities, there stands the cathedral. Somehow the fact that far higher buildings may now soar above it seems not to detract from it. True, the height of the cathedrals may be far exceeded, but in a way that is difficult to describe, the cathedrals are not diminished. I can only presume that what they communicate is a kind of massiveness, a resilience, a stubborn and silent continuation.

From time to time this silence is broken by their bells. Even this sound has a singularity about it. That singularity allows it to be heard above the myriad sounds of the technological city. The bells of the cathedrals pierce not sharply but gently, with an easy mellow richness that does not intrude but is impossible to ignore. Listening to the bell of an old cathedral makes you aware of time in a way that no computer, no harsh blast, no radio announcement can do. Standing in the shadow of St Stephen's Cathedral in Vienna, a light rain glistening on the open area around it, I am about to move out again into the heart of the city when suddenly the bell tolls the early afternoon hour. The sound cascades down among the buildings. There is a rushing and fluttering of wings as pigeons respond before settling down again. The sounds of the city, enveloped for a moment by the bells' voice, return. I have been made aware of the time. But also by the bell I have somehow been made aware of a quality of existence deeper than time.

Cathedral

As you visit the great cathedrals of Europe these days you have all the various reactions that visitors have always had. There is of course the vastness of the enterprise. Even today, when most cities have changed rapidly and reared great highrise monuments to modern priorities, the cathedrals of Europe still refuse to be dwarfed. If not by height certainly by weight of history and tradition, coupled with their elaboration and design, they have retained their significance.

Inside they communicate what they were designed to do. To enter is instinctively to look up. Almost everybody who enters, however weary they are from the tourist trek, however weighted by cameras, their first instinct is to look up. This of course is exactly what the master craftsmen of long ago intended.

There is a modern equivalent. I can recall in a photograph seeing a line of rocket launchers standing idle, their great barrels or columns vertical, ready to blast off their contents to the skies. Look at these great cathedrals and you see exactly the same thing. Every pillar soars from its stone foundations to the roof far above; every stained glass window, long and slim, points upward. They too long ago were designed not to lift fire and death and steel into the sky, but to lift the human mind and soul to levels of reality beyond and around everyday reality. For nearly a thousand years they have done this, and they show every sign of doing it for a thousand more.

Epidaurus

There is the avenue of trees, the wild flowers, the song of birds, the sudden emergence into the sunlit stage area. All this I recall so vividly from Epidaurus in southern Greece. The wonder of Epidaurus is the number of things it once was. All of them brought together can be summed up in the word "healing" or "therapy."

Around the fifth century BC this was a centre where men and women came in their thousands. With them they brought all the things that affect us as human beings, ailments mental, physical, psychological. The very fact that I list our ailments in categories reveals me as a twentieth century western man. The fact that I question my own categorizing reveals me as a twentieth century man of the 1980s. In recent years we have been drawn again by a thought, an insight, a tantalising possibility tempting us, to think that all human illness — physical, mental, psychological, spiritual — is much more of a connected fabric than we had tended to think. I have deliberately described this insight as a tantalizing possibility because we will never understand the one great thread that leads us to the heart of the human condition and thus gives us a God-like power to cure our many inter-connected illnesses. But even now the insight has at least affected medical attitudes. More and more we are realizing that many illnesses arise out of the infinitely complex total being that each one of us is. As we form and deepen this insight, it is salutory to stand at Epidaurus and to realize that men pursued the same insight twenty-five centuries ago.

Between Two Worlds

There are certain places that are conducive to thought. If you drive north from Kowloon, into the New Territories, you eventually find yourself at the border of the People's Republic of China. At one point the road ends in a widened area where you can, if you wish, turn about. If you go on, you come to a barricade. Beyond the barricade the road slopes slightly up hill until it disappears over the hill. Beyond that dip is China.

I know that in some ways China is not the enigma it was. It has become almost mandatory for aspiring political figures to visit Peking. Every week companies send their upper management to visit China. And yet with it all, the feelings, inner life, motivations, and hopes of this vast land are still largely unknown to us. Here in this ancient civilization my western kind has left a bad track record. Rarely have we come for other than exploitation, although men and women with absolute sincerity have laid their bones in China, because they came in love and hope.

I can only say what I thought of as we stood looking from south to north. I thought of the endless dilemma that every society has to wrestle with. What is primary, the freedom of the individual or the welfare of the totality? And since no choice can be absolute, where is the balance to be found between the choices our two worlds have made? I thought also of the growing realization in the West that life in the future simply has to be more social and more communal.

Already we have had to curb individual freedom to a degree we don't notice because it is gradual. How will that future society be formed, which the earth needs so badly if we are to survive? Will it be formed as this China was, in agony and revolution and with terrible human cost, or will there be a sharing and a reaching for justice through a growing awareness and sensitivity in our western world? To look at the distant mountains of China is to ask many questions.

Children of Two Worlds

In Hong Kong, between the great wall of highrises that face the water and the water itself, there is a wide heavily trafficked boulevard that is crossed at a couple of places by pedestrian bridges. When you cross, at least where I did, you are quite near one of the many harbour sections that serve different purposes. This particular section of water is a kind of floating image of the modern world.

First, in near the harbour wall to my left and right, there are the sampans. They are clustered together, moving slightly as the people move hither and yon from boat to boat. They form a dark coloured huddled mass on the water. Now and again a sampan will detach itself and move out among the lines and off into the great bay. There is a constant busyness, a ceaseless lifting of sacks and boxes, washing is hung to dry, children play. Obviously it is a little world, a community.

Beyond the huddled sampans you look over the outer part of this stretch of water. In front of you, gleaming white and chrome, reflecting the sun, riding at anchor, are scores of ocean going private luxury craft.

I suppose the reason the scene registered with me was because of a fleeting image I noticed. A sampan had detached itself and was threading its way out into the harbour. Standing at the bow was a small child. I'd say she was about four or five. And as the sampan passed beside one of these gleaming pleasure craft, another child appeared on its deck. Again, a small girl not very much older. For a moment they stood, only about twenty feet apart, and looked at each other until the sampan passed around the yacht's bow and headed out. As I turned away I felt that I had seen a symbol of the worlds that intersect here and elsewhere, and that will not go on for ever . . .

En Route to Asia

I am perfectly certain that really to enjoy travel you have to be a romantic at heart. To savour travel you have to be ready to see reality as more than itself, to see things with what some people call "the third eye."

All day long I have lived in this airplane. This morning I left Vancouver, and two hours later I saw one of the wonders of the world. I looked down on what so many see as just another chunk of California real-estate. But I was really looking down on one of the most dramatic pieces of the earth, the San Andreas fault, poised on the edge of a continent, some day, people say, to move with unimaginable terror and majesty toward the ocean.

Or again, at some moment on this day I changed the very day itself. Silently, imperceptibly, Monday became Tuesday in a strange twist of time that is not time. I have "lost," as we say, a day.

And yet again, I have done today what a prophet of old did in a mythical story. I read of Jonah crossing the ancient Mediterranean in the belly of a whale. That is precisely what I have done in a new kind of ocean and a new and wondrous technological whale called a 747 Pan American clipper!

And there are more miracles and wonders on this day in my life. At least one. I read of Joshua for whom, it is said, in that ancient biblical war the sun stood still. And lo, this day for me the sun, if not standing still, has slowed his journey across the sky until he seemed almost to have stood and waited for my great chariot. A day of wonders and miracles. But look, three seats from me is a man plugged in to the movie. Alas, nothing on the screen is half as wonderful as the reality he is missing!

Seasons

The cycle of the year, as we all well know, is not just a geophysical process to which we come as observers. We do not observe winter or spring. We feel them deep down inside ourselves. Their shadows and shafts of light move across our interior countryside, dictating and shaping our moods, our feelings, our responses. Each year in this Journal, I find the seasons asking for some expression. Each year I obey.

Mount Baker

A day of beauty, at least a day begun and ended in beauty. The kind of thing not easy to put into words, but there is a longing to . . .

Early in the morning, a Saturday. Not a Saturday open and free for whatever I choose to do. I have made a commitment to a group of people on Friday night and most of this Saturday.

The early morning in the city is cold and dry and, at this early hour, silent. The car engine splits the silence, and one moves down the street with some guilt. Moving south-east, the north shore mountains stand at the far ends of the major intersections as I cross them. They wear that mingling of blue and grey and white that seems to be taken on by both mountains and oceans in the months of their wintering.

Moving out now beyond the city. Little traffic as yet. The first fields with a silken like sheen on their green grass as they wait for the sun. Through the flashing kaleidoscope of the Deas tunnel. I always feel they should have quadrophonic speakers all through that tunnel playing either Orpheus in the Underworld or the overture to William Tell!

Suddenly, as if vast curtains had been swept aside to set a Wagnerian scene, there is Mount Baker, every curve and crevice vivid and clear, its white crown flashing and glinting, and behind it the sky flaming with what I can describe only as a cauldron of colour. Delicate pink to rose to scarlet, changing and merging even as I look at them and drive toward that distant loveliness. No wonder those who galloped across this wooded estuary five thousand years ago worshipped this mountain. I, hurtling along in my steel cocoon, a child of their distant future, come to worship also . . .

Morning Lake

First there is the grass beyond the verandah, after that the few feet of gravelly sand that slopes gently into the water. Later in the day the sand will burn the soles of one's feet, but now, soon after dawn, it is cool and fresh and welcoming. All night the lake was disturbed by a wind that came out of the south west. It was not a storm but enough to send the lake into a choppy and angry dance which now laps and slops against the dock and breaks on the beach hour after hour.

Now the wind has gone, and the only traces are some leaves and small branches lying around. The lake is totally still. It is curious how the stillness of a great body of water has such a capacity to rivet one's attention. You look at it, your eyes moving quickly from the familiar shallows out to where you can no longer see the bottom, then far out into the depths you can only guess at, a great foreign country, shadowed, silent, hiding things covered for ten thousand years.

Here and there are patches of mist on the water, whimsically captured by the lake's different areas of warmth and cold. I am reminded of such a mist, manufactured and carefully designed, pouring across the stage as the lovely music of Tchaikowsky moves me toward the climax of *Swan Lake* in a remembered theatre. These wisps of mist on the lake herald no actors, no diversion for the mind. They emphasize instead silence, tranquillity. They lull one into contemplation about that little play of one's own life. It lies, as most of our lives do, in the great densely populated middle zone that is neither comedy nor tragedy. Yet here on this inner stage of my life, as of yours, are all the ingredients of drama, love, hope, anxiety, wonder, and much more. The ingredients of our humanity that you and I share by this morning lake.

Generation

When does spring come? Well, it comes officially as a date on a calendar. It comes when the shop windows declare that it is here by showing us clothes that make what we are wearing look dowdy. And we stand torn between desire and shock as we look at the appalling figures, written in a deliberately cheerful and playful script, on the price labels.

But none of that is really spring. Spring comes on the day when you become aware that there is a new batch of children on the street, children who were invisible during the winter and who suddenly emerge for their first mobile, adventuring, laughing spring time. This happens on streets. You join a street, and your children play on it, and time and years go by. Now and again furniture vans come to other houses, and there is a move out and a move in, a tree is cut down here and a house is painted there. From time to time vague faces are noticed, and sometimes there are signs that a family is obviously expecting a new addition.

Then one day there is a flood of warmth and sun across the roofs and gardens and distant mountains, and you realize that your suit needs dry cleaning and the house windows need washing, and along the street there are two small forms crouched behind a tree, obviously hoping that you won't point them out to the two other tiny forms tottering around in search of them in a game of hide and seek. Somebody else tiny is standing eye to eye with a dog and hanging onto its ear watching the others who can walk and run, not being quite sure whether he himself can set out across the grass without coming a cropper.

You watch this new set of beings emerge from the walls of winter, from the cocoon of home. You realize that they will always recall these first mornings of a new spring. For them every tree is immeasurably tall and majestic, and every hour of play is endless. So it should be. So it will always be.

Deer

Very early in the morning. High summer on Vancouver Island. The sun, still seen through trees, pouring along the far edges of the world, dispensing the gifts of a king. The air is totally still. The sounds and movements of life betray themselves only if you stand still and send out all your attention. Then you begin to see the activity, to hear the stirring. The first insect moving near your feet, the shimmer of a web stretched with deceptive fragility between the branches, the first sounds of the new day from sheep in the next pasture, still unseen through the high hedge. Then beyond them, other sounds creep in as the last minutes of early morning are invaded by a waking world. Sound from another farm, a solitary car going toward the distant highway, as yet no voices.

I am standing on a slight slope. It is really a long hill, once heavily wooded before this area was domesticated and the trees felled and the boundaries marked. In the distance is the small bay. I turn and look up the slope to where the trees still stand. Up through them is a winding path to a clearing, and there, totally still and utterly silent, stand two deer. They stand in a pool of morning sunlight, and they look down through the darkened pathway to where I stand. I too, keep absolutely still. For a long moment we share this morning world. We gaze at one another, fellow creatures of the sun and this green and lovely world. We gaze at each other down corridors of time and creation. Suddenly they wheel about and the clearing is empty, their going as silent and instantaneous as their coming. I am alone again in a world made wondrous between sleeping and waking.

Labour Day

The evening of Monday, the last day of the Labour Day weekend. In a way a lovely evening. Its sky and air define this time of year. The sun is emerging from gentle showers, sailing across blue spaces of sky only to disappear again. The rain is not winter rain, yet neither is it a summer shower. After the drenching there will not be the rising steam that a summer sun can bring from the earth. The air is not winter, yet neither is it summer. Air, sky, light, everything is poised between two moments, two moods, two kinds of beauty. The time of year, at least this particular moment on this Monday of Labour Day weekend, is like the moment when the orchestra has left the stage after playing the music of summer. The stage is there, the instruments are everywhere, yet the music remains only in the echoes of the mind.

There are echoes at this time of the year, different for each one of us, but the same music and the same themes. There is a moment when you turn a bend in the Fraser Canyon and see the first distant glimpse of the far away Chilcotin-Cariboo country. There is the realization of the force and the majestic grandeur of a prairie storm in thunder and lightning. There is a meeting with a face and a voice one had not met for almost twenty years, and an easy feeling of being able to continue the relationship as if a conversation had just been left off. There is a drive in a truck down a valley far in from the highway among the mountains, moving through early morning farms and the mist not yet fully gone. There is the realization that one's family has got taller.

Thoughts as summer is ending and the world changes into the garments of autumn.

November

These are the days when two stages of the year's cycle blend and live together for a while. In the back garden, seen from the den window, the last of the leaves have just gone from the trees. At the end of the garden there is a big mound of them, still valiantly trying to be golden and bronze even in death.

Far away, also seen in glimpses between the houses from the same window, the distant water and the mountains beyond are dallying, as yet only dallying with their next love affair. They have dressed themselves in blue and green for summer. They have changed to brown and gold for their autumn love. Now as they await the first coming of winter, they are already donning white mantles, and around their lower slopes, the greys and sombre shades of these shortening days are beginning to appear.

Even though the official weekends of burning leaves are long gone, there is still the courageous (or desperate) law breaker who sends a silent furtive column of smoke into the suburban air, trusting that, by its very solitariness, it will not provoke neighbourly or official retaliation. Sometimes on a clear and lovely day the great machines, heaving and lurching and fussing around the streets like snorting housekeeprs critical of the inhabitants, come with their great brushes and try to sweep away the last of the leaves at the kerbside. They shuffle and lurch in and out between the parked cars, and go away frustrated. When for the last time they go, you know that all pretence of fall is gone. One is now on one's own. If the leaves have not been raked, so be it. Like a foolish biblical virgin, you must go out to meet the bridegroom of winter with your lamps untrimmed . . .

Ramble

It was a very simple journey, rather short, but taking it was one of those things that sometimes remain vividly in the mind after a holiday.

The house is on the side of a small valley, and there are woods behind and a gravelled road in front. The world here is full of slow things, if you know what I mean. Smoke seems to go up slowly from a chimney, infrequently a solitary slow-moving car passes on the road, animal or bird noises sound in the near distance. You can hear the faint fall of rain on a thousand trees and bushes and a million leaves. Near the house there is a small creek, and it has a voice that never ceases.

We climb up the wet soft paths to the hilltop behind the house, to where the slope levels for a while before going upward again. Further up there, patches of mist lie among the dark trees. From somewhere in that quietness and loneliness the creek begins its journey toward us. It comes out of the trees, small, chattery, fussing over mossy stones and fallen branches, and it passes by where we are standing. From there, because we have rubber boots, we follow it.

It crosses the little plateau where we stand above the house, and then it cascades over a steep narrow waterfall where we climb down, trying not to slip and at the same time laughing about our efforts. At the bottom of the narrow cleft we splash through the little pool and then follow further until the stream passes the house and goes diving under the road. Perhaps in summer time somebody small could go into the mysterious tunnel with light at the other end, but not now. So we cross the road and re-enter the trees. Sliding and splashing and saying silly things, we come to the end of the woods. The stream says good bye as it flows into a silent and dark tidal creek; in turn we head for home.

A simple thing but a lovely thing to be remembered . . .

St Michael and All Angels

If I said to you that today is the feast of St Michael and All Angels, what would go through your mind? I ask the question because for millions of people that statement would have about it a kind of medieval ring. Putting it mildly, it isn't likely to be part of casual conversation in, let us say, a lineup at the airport tomorrow!

Yet by losing what such a day means we lose something valuable and beautiful. In other centuries, before Mr and Mrs Freud of Vienna brought forth their son Sigmund, people experienced all the gamut of emotions and thoughts for which today we have psychiatric terms. Then, in those previous centuries, when people wished to express the fact that they had experienced something of particular intensity, when they wished to speak of something that had struck them very forcibly and directed them in a certain way, or had made them change their life in some way, or warned them at some deep level of their being in some danger, or had suddenly given them a blinding insight into some aspect of life — when anything like that became part of their experience, they would say quite matter-of-factly that an angel had visited them.

When a Greek or Roman poet or playwright spoke of his work as coming from a muse, he was saying the same thing. Was this silly or naive? Was it something to be smiled at pityingly by enlightened moderns? I don't think so at all. I cannot help noticing that the more resolutely we dismiss angels from our minds, the more neurotically we fill theatres, movies, and paperbacks with demons. Maybe someone is trying to tell us something. I wonder who?

Eine Kleine Nachtmusic

Of all seasons of the year this is the time when the Fraser Canyon impresses. Later on in the depth of winter it will be more stark. The snow, new fallen on the ageless rock, will show jagged contrasts of black and white. But on those same days there will be, unless of course it is actually blizzarding, a brightness. The peaks against the sky will blaze out. Now and again there will be the odd glimpse of a distant horizon, equally snow laden, gleaming white far across the Chilcotin plateau.

But at this time of year, in this season of the dying of the last spirits of late autumn, when the passing of an evening hour brings first the shadows and then the darkness swooping down the sides of the canyon, these are the evenings when the canyon is elemental, dangerous, unforgiving. The sky lies along the mountains, trailing wisps into the crevasses, suddenly becoming fog in the headlights of the car, and then retreating again just as suddenly. The river is black and churning. Driving the canyon highway one hurries through a vast darkening cathedral of nature, the headlights of approaching cars hurtling past like votive candles lit against the fearful darkness.

As night comes I put on a tape, and I listen to Mozart's *Eine Kleine Nachtmusic,* and I suddenly realize the utter contrast. Here in my ears is that ultimate precision and order so beloved of a century that in its time wished to order the universe, both nature and humanity, to order it into neat, predictable patterns. Outside me in the darkness is nature refusing to be ordered, nature instead vast and terrible and shadowed. The music, I suspect, is my unconscious defence against that encroaching chaos. It's interesting why I reached for that particular tape. I am uncomfortable before a dark majesty that is beyond my ordering. I am in the presence of something awesome.

Notch Hill

We usually drive far more highways than we do roads. Roads are intimate and local. Roads meander. Roads pause for things. They run under deep trees and let shadows play on their surfaces. Roads go down by small rivers, even streams. Really intimate and quiet roads sometimes give way to a stream and allow it to cross them. Travellers slow down and the water splashes from the wheels. Roads allow houses to be close to them and animals to saunter across them.

Highways are different. Highways are restless and assertive. They are never-endingly bossy. Not a mile goes by but they are hurling information at you. Yield! No U-turns! No gasoline for 75 kilometres! Highways flatten out hills and roar over rivers. Highways dislike houses and push them hundreds of yards to either side. Highways detest trees and human beings and small communities.

I am thinking of a certain road into the hills which leaves the highway far behind. It climbs a ridge and then drops into a rich and fertile valley. There are farms where already half a day's chores are done even as we drive slowly by. Someone waves a greeting, and there is a store with nails and bread and ice cream among other jumbled things. Across the fields there is an old wooden church with a tiny bell tower and gaping windows. From the step where the door once was we can see the long shimmering steel of the railroad that once halted here but now instead goes thundering ponderously through this valley, bound for places perhaps more important but, alas, not half as beautiful.